The Integrated Curriculum

The Integrated Curriculum

Books for Reluctant Readers, Grades 2–5

SECOND EDITION

Anthony D. Fredericks

Illustrated by
Anthony Allan Stoner

1998
Teacher Ideas Press
A Division of
Libraries Unlimited, Inc.
Englewood, Colorado

To Roxanne Myers for bounteous sharing,
warm friendship, and celebrated camaraderie.

TEACHER IDEAS PRESS
A Division of
Libraries Unlimited, Inc.
P.O. Box 6633
Englewood, CO 80155-6633
1-800-237-6124
www.lu.com/tip

Production Editor: Kevin W. Perizzolo
Copy Editor: Diane Hess
Proofreader: Felicity Tucker
Indexer: Lee Brower
Typesetter: Kay Minnis

Library of Congress Cataloging-in-Publication Data

Fredericks, Anthony D.
    The integrated curriculum : books for reluctant readers, grades
2-5 / Anthony D. Fredericks ; illustrated by Anthony Allan Stoner --
2nd ed.
    xiii, 189 p. 22x28 cm.
    Includes bibliographical references and index.
    ISBN 1-56308-604-2 (softbound)
    1. Reading (Elementary)--United States--Language experience
approach--Handbooks, manuals, etc. 2. Interdisciplinary approach in
education--United States--Handbooks, manuals, etc. 3. Language
arts--Correlation with content subjects--United States--Handbooks,
manuals, etc. 4. Children--United States--Books and reading.
I. Title. II. Stoner, Anthony Allan
LB1573.33.F74   1998
372.62--dc21   98-25912
                                                        CIP

Contents

Preface xi

Acknowledgments xiii

PART 1
Motivation, Connection,
and Comprehension

MOTIVATION:
Gold Stars and Smelly Stickers . . . 1
Give Students Choices. 3
Provide Recreational Reading . . . 5
Promote a Whole-Classroom
Approach to Reading 5
Build Strong Ties to School
and Public Libraries 5
Make Reading Literature Based . . 5
Model Appropriate Reading
Behaviors 6
Create an Atmosphere of High
Expectations 6
Meet Students' Needs 6
Emphasize Process over Product,
Strategies over Skills. 6
Use Whole Texts Rather Than
Language Fragments. 6

CONNECTION:
Building an Integrated
Curriculum 7
Make Reading Cross-Curricular . . 7
Integrate the Language Arts
Throughout the Curriculum . . 7
Integrate Language and
Language Use into
Every Curricular Area 7
Integrate Students' Interests
and Needs with Aims of
the Curriculum 8
Engage Students in Real-World
Activities 8
Book Extensions. 8
Additional Projects. 11

PARTICIPATORY
COMPREHENSION:
Processes (Not Panaceas)
for Reluctant Readers 16
Student-Generated Questions . . . 16
MM&M (Metacognitive Modeling
and Monitoring) 18
Prediction Cards 20
K-W-L. 22
Anticipation Guide 24
Reflective Sharing Technique . . . 26
Character Continuum 28

PART 2
Bookwebbing Techniques
and Activities

USING CHILDREN'S
LITERATURE
ACROSS THE CURRICULUM . . . 35

Grade 2

Bugs (Parker and Wright) 39
Summary 39
Critical Thinking Questions 39
Reading/Language Arts 40
Science/Health 40
Art 40
Math 41
Music 41
Social Studies 41
Physical Education. 41

Frog and Toad Are Friends
(Lobel) 42
Summary 42
Critical Thinking Questions 42
Reading/Language Arts 42
Science/Health 42
Art 43
Math 43
Music 44
Social Studies 44
Physical Education. 45

I Know an Old Lady (Bonne) 46
Summary 46
Critical Thinking Questions 46
Reading/Language Arts 46
Science/Health 47
Art 48
Math 48
Music 48
Social Studies 49
Physical Education 49

Jack and the Beanstalk
(Cauley) 50
Summary 50
Critical Thinking Questions . . . 50
Reading/Language Arts 50
Science/Health 51
Art 51
Math 51
Music 52
Social Studies 52
Physical Education 53

Leo the Late Bloomer (Kraus) 54
Summary 54
Critical Thinking Questions 54
Reading/Language Arts 54
Science/Health 54
Art 55
Math 56
Music 56
Social Studies 56
Physical Education 56

The Three Bears (Galdone) 57
Summary 57
Critical Thinking Questions . . . 57
Reading/Language Arts 57
Science/Health 58
Art 58
Math 58
Music 58
Social Studies 59
Physical Education 59

The Very Hungry Caterpillar
(Carle) 60
Summary 60
Critical Thinking Questions 60
Reading/Language Arts 60
Science/Health 60
Art 61
Math 61
Music 62
Social Studies 62
Physical Education 62

The Yucky Reptile Alphabet
Book (Pallotta) 63
Summary 63
Critical Thinking Questions 63
Reading/Language Arts 63
Science/Health 64
Art 64
Math 64
Music 65
Social Studies 65
Physical Education 65

Grade 3

Alexander and the Terrible,
Horrible, No Good,
Very Bad Day (Viorst) 66
Summary 66
Critical Thinking Questions 66
Reading/Language Arts 66
Science/Health 67
Art 67
Math 68
Music 68
Social Studies 68
Physical Education 68

The Bathwater Gang (Spinelli) . . . 69
Summary 69
Critical Thinking Questions 69
Reading/Language Arts 69
Science/Health 70
Art 70
Math 70
Music 71
Social Studies 71
Physical Education 71

Cow (Older). 72
   Summary 72
   Critical Thinking Questions 72
   Reading/Language Arts 72
   Hey, Diddle, Diddle, the Cat and
      the Fiddle, and the Cow Just
      Can't Get over the Moon
      (script) 73
   Science/Health 75
   Art 75
   Math 76
   Music 76
   Social Studies 76
   Physical Education. 76

The Day Jimmy's Boa Ate the
      Wash (Noble) 77
   Summary 77
   Critical Thinking Questions . . . 77
   Reading/Language Arts 77
   Science/Health 78
   Art 78
   Math 79
   Music 79
   Social Studies 79
   Physical Education. 79

Dinosaurs: Strange and
      Wonderful (Pringle) 80
   Summary 80
   Critical Thinking Questions 80
   Reading/Language Arts 81
   Science/Health 81
   Art 82
   Math 82
   Music 83
   Social Studies 83
   Physical Education. 83

The Flunking of Joshua T.
      Bates (Shreve). 84
   Summary 84
   Critical Thinking Questions 84
   Reading/Language Arts 84
   Science/Health 85
   Art 85
   Math 86
   Music 86
   Social Studies 86
   Physical Education. 87

Ira Sleeps Over (Waber) 88
   Summary 88
   Critical Thinking Questions 88
   Reading/Language Arts 88
   Science/Health 88
   Art 89
   Math 89
   Music 89
   Social Studies 89
   Physical Education. 89

Miss Nelson Is Missing! (Allard) . . . 90
   Summary 90
   Critical Thinking Questions 90
   Reading/Language Arts 90
   Science/Health 91
   Art 91
   Math 91
   Music 91
   Social Studies 92
   Physical Education. 92

The Salamander Room (Mazer) . . . 93
   Summary 93
   Critical Thinking Questions 93
   Reading/Language Arts 93
   Science/Health 94
   Art 95
   Math 95
   Music 95
   Social Studies 96
   Physical Education. 96

Grade 4

Cloudy with a Chance of
      Meatballs (Barrett). 97
   Summary 97
   Critical Thinking Questions 97
   Reading/Language Arts 97
   Science/Health 98
   Art 100
   Math. 100
   Music 100
   Social Studies 101
   Physical Education 101

***East of the Sun and West of
      the Moon*** (Mayer) 102
   Summary 102
   Critical Thinking Questions . . . 102
   Reading/Language Arts. 102
   Science/Health 103
   Art 104
   Math. 104
   Music 105
   Social Studies 105
   Physical Education 105

The Great Kapok Tree (Cherry) . . 106
   Summary 106
   Critical Thinking Questions . . . 106
   Reading/Language Arts. 106
   Science/Health 107
   Art 107
   Math. 107
   Music 107
   Social Studies 108
   Physical Education 108

***Mufaro's Beautiful
      Daughters*** (Steptoe) 109
   Summary 109
   Critical Thinking Questions . . . 109
   Reading/Language Arts. 110
   Science/Health 110
   Art 111
   Math. 111
   Music 112
   Social Studies 112
   Physical Education 112

Sky Tree (Locker) 113
   Summary 113
   Critical Thinking Questions . . . 113
   Reading/Language Arts. 113
   Science/Health 114
   Art 114
   Math. 115
   Music 116
   Social Studies 116
   Physical Education 116

Surprising Swimmers
      (Fredericks). 117
   Summary 117
   Critical Thinking Questions . . . 117
   Reading/Language Arts. 117
   Science/Health 118
   Art 119
   Math. 119
   Music 120
   Social Studies 120
   Physical Education 120

***The True Story of the 3 Little
      Pigs*** (Scieszka). 121
   Summary 121
   Critical Thinking Questions . . . 121
   Reading/Language Arts. 121
   *The Really Really Really True
      Story of the Three Little
      Pigs* (script). 122
   Science/Health 126
   Art 126
   Math. 127
   Music 127
   Social Studies 127
   Physical Education 127

Volcanoes (Simon) 128
   Summary 128
   Critical Thinking Questions . . . 128
   Reading/Language Arts. 128
   Science/Health 128
   Art 129
   Math. 129
   Music 130
   Social Studies 130
   Physical Education 130

The Wednesday Surprise
      (Bunting) 131
   Summary 131
   Critical Thinking Questions . . . 131
   Reading/Language Arts. 131
   Science/Health 132
   Art 132
   Math. 132
   Music 133
   Social Studies 133
   Physical Education 133

Grade 5

Clever Camouflagers

(Fredericks). 134
Summary 134
Critical Thinking Questions . . . 134
Reading/Language Arts. 134
Science/Health 135
Art. 136
Math. 136
Music 136
Social Studies 137
Physical Education 137

Dear Mr. Henshaw (Cleary). . . . 138

Summary 138
Critical Thinking Questions . . . 138
Reading/Language Arts. 138
Science/Health 139
Art. 139
Math. 139
Music 140
Social Studies 140
Physical Education 140

Jeremy Thatcher, Dragon Hatcher (Coville) 141

Summary 141
Critical Thinking Questions . . . 141
Reading/Language Arts. 141
Science/Health 142
Art. 143
Math. 143
Music 143
Social Studies 143
Physical Education 143

More Scary Stories to Tell in the Dark (Schwartz) 144

Summary 144
Critical Thinking Questions . . . 144
Reading/Language Arts. 144
Science/Health 145
Art. 145
Math. 145
Music 146
Social Studies 146
Physical Education 146

My Side of the Mountain

(George). 147
Summary 147
Critical Thinking Questions . . . 147
Reading/Language Arts. 147
Science/Health 148
Art. 148
Math. 149
Music 149
Social Studies 149
Physical Education 150

Sadako and the Thousand Paper Cranes (Coerr). . . . 151

Summary 151
Critical Thinking Questions . . . 151
Reading/Language Arts. 151
Science/Health 152
Art. 153
Math. 153
Music 153
Social Studies 154
Physical Education 154

Tales of a Fourth Grade Nothing (Blume) 155

Summary 155
Critical Thinking Questions . . . 155
Reading/Language Arts. 155
Science/Health 155
Art. 156
Math. 156
Music 157
Social Studies 157
Physical Education 157

Where the Buffaloes Begin

(Baker). 158
Summary 158
Critical Thinking Questions . . . 158
Reading/Language Arts. 158
Science/Health 159
Art. 159
Math. 160
Music 160
Social Studies 160
Physical Education 160

The Whipping Boy (Fleischman) . . 161
    Summary 161
    Critical Thinking Questions . . . 161
    Reading/Language Arts. 161
    Science/Health 162
    Art 162
    Math 162
    Music 163
    Social Studies 163
    Physical Education 164

PART 3
Resources

**RECOMMENDED SUPPLEMENTAL
CHILDREN'S LITERATURE** . . . 165
    Grades 1–2 166
    Grades 3–4 169
    Grades 5–6 173

WEB SITES 177

    Index 179
    About the Author 189

Preface

I guess I've always been a reader. When I got my first flashlight as a kid, I would crawl under the covers at night to read the latest Hardy Boys mystery or Tarzan adventure. Later, in high school, my teachers would mention to my parents that I needed to spend more time with my textbooks and less time with the novels in the school library. Now, as an adult, I am still a voracious reader—reading everything including business books, education texts, science books, novels, travelogues, books on writing, magazines and professional journals, humor, and even cartoons.

When I was growing up in southern California our home was filled with books on every subject. My parents were readers too; they subscribed to magazines and book clubs, were ardent readers of the *Los Angeles Times*, and shared what they learned during dinner table conversations. As my first role models, they showed me the enjoyment and information that can come from books.

I was fortunate to attend schools where books and literature were prized. St. Matthew's School in Pacific Palisades, California, and the Orme School in Mayer, Arizona, made reading a high priority in every course. Textbooks were frequently supplemented with required readings in the library, courses were enhanced with lists of supplemental books, and reading the "classics" during the summer months was strongly encouraged. My elementary and high school years were filled with books and literature and opportunities to share them with classmates and teachers in a variety of ways. (I suspect that my intensely literate background was a major impetus in my decision to become a teacher.)

The Integrated Curriculum: Books for Reluctant Readers, Grades 2–5 (second edition) grew out of my own experiences as a student constantly surrounded by books and my work as a classroom teacher in helping youngsters develop positive attitudes and skills in reading. This book also grew out of conversations with colleagues around the country who are concerned about the growing legion of students in their classrooms who can read but are "choosing" not to. These reluctant readers may be influenced by many factors including parental attitudes and choices, peer pressure, teachers as role models, self-concepts, and cultural and societal perceptions of reading.

However, this book is not intended as an exposé on the causes of this "problem" but rather as a celebration of quality literature as a significant part of every course and every student's life. I sincerely hope that you and your students discover a host of energizing ideas for your reading program within the pages of this book. I wish you well in your quest to help reluctant readers become eager readers!

—Tony Fredericks

Acknowledgments

For encouragement and support throughout the writing of the second edition of this book I am particularly indebted to the following:

To Kevin W. Perizzolo, the editor on this edition, goes accolades and commendations for marshaling the manuscript through the maze of production details and unbelievable deadlines.

To Maxwell House for producing the magic elixir of all writers—rich Colombian coffee!

To my dog, Sienna, and her frequent visits to my office during early morning drafting and late night editing. She always had a patient and non-judgmental "third ear" for all manner of creative musings.

To all my students at York College who consistently provide me with a plethora of possibilities and an abundance of spirit—may their careers be filled with equal cheer and jubilation.

To the thousands of teachers around the country who have logged on to my Web site—http://www.afredericks.com—and unselfishly shared their ideas, thoughts, and incredible classroom experiences in every curricular area. May this book reflect their creativity and determination in helping every child succeed—in school and in life!

MOTIVATION:
Gold Stars and Smelly Stickers

When I was in the sixth grade my teacher, Mrs. MacDonald, posted an oversized chart in a front corner of the classroom. On the chart she listed every student's name down the left-hand side. Next to each name Mrs. MacDonald would place a colored star depending on how one did on the weekly spelling test. The object, I suppose, was to publicly recognize those who had mastered the spelling words for the week and to provide an incentive for those who were less than adequate spellers.

I have never been and will never be a great speller. In fact, I believe that one of the greatest technological advances in the past fifty years (ranking far ahead of astronauts landing on the moon and microwave ovens) is the spell checker on my word processing program. That single feature has done more to advance my writing career and eliminate my concerns over "i before e, except after c" and other spelling peccadilloes than any other discovery or invention of this century. It is my saving grace and my professional life preserver.

In sixth grade my spelling was considerably worse than it is now. While my classmates were accumulating stars of every size and color, I lagged far behind (imagine my distress on parent–teacher night when my lack of spelling prowess went on public display). My best friend, in contrast, was the spelling wizard of sixth grade and was accorded the honor of having two horizontal rows assigned to his name because of the sheer number of gold stars he had accumulated over the course of the year. By June I still had only three blue stars!

Even today, I can picture that chart. I am still aware of how I felt about the public display of my spelling deficits. I am also aware that the chart in no way encouraged me to become a better speller. Rather, it may have been more of a hindrance to my spelling development than Mrs. MacDonald would have ever thought possible.

Now, with more than 28 years of teaching experience, I have come to the conclusion that as teachers, we must provide opportunities for our students to develop their own internal sense of motivation instead of "controlling" them through external means. Awarding gold stars and smelly stickers fosters a competitive approach to learning, and there is a growing legion of educators who believe that competitive goal structures tend to heighten student anxiety and avoidance reactions, promote group fragmentation and hostility, and subvert the development of an intrinsic motivation for learning.

Simply stated, motivation is of two types. With *extrinsic* motivation, one person has control over another person or an individual relies on others to establish personal goals and the reward system for meeting those goals. With *intrinsic* motivation, in contrast, drive and ambition are determined internally, that is, an individual sets his or her own goals and feels empowered to pursue them. As you might expect, logic and research support the notion that intrinsically motivated students do better academically than extrinsically motivated students. Specifically:

1. Extrinsically motivated students are engaged in a competitive atmosphere that becomes self-defeating in the long run.

2. "External" students work only for rewards. The queries "What grade did I get?" and "How did I do?" are typical indicators of extrinsic students. Thus, motivation to learn is subverted at the expense of reward accumulation, the relationship between effort and achievement is not apparent, and process is not valued.

3. Creativity and problem-solving activities are avoided in favor of low-level thinking activities.

4. Goals, if any, are short term and immediate. Long-range projects and thinking are avoided by extrinsic students.

5. Extrinsic students do not take personal responsibility for their learning but rather see the things that happen to them as a matter of luck or chance.

6. "Externalizing" becomes a self-perpetuating cycle for extrinsic students in which continual lack of academic success substantiates a belief that one may never be successful.

Because there is a strong relationship between motivation and academic achievement, we need to be mindful of the behaviors we exercise in the classroom that can lead to heightened levels of motivation and, in turn, heightened levels of achievement. This awareness becomes even more critical when we work with reluctant readers. Because many teachers promote reading as the "universal subject" (as does society in general) students, from very early in their educational careers, learn that reading competence is a strong determinant of academic competence in general. Thus both educators and students perceive a lack of success or a reluctance to engage in literacy activities as a serious impediment to total scholastic growth.

Many educators believe that students do not become reluctant readers solely as a result of below-average intelligence, adverse socioeconomic conditions, or lack of materials. Instead, students' reluctance to read is often due to the instruction (or lack of instruction) they receive in the classroom. In short, it could be said that readers are made, not born.

I support the idea that the teacher is the preeminent force (along with parents) in a child's approach to and progress in reading. The way we approach reading in the classroom, both intellectually and affectively, is critical to how much children embrace reading as a natural and normal part of their everyday lives. In my own classrooms I found that too many children saw reading as a school-related or classroom-only activity. That is, many kids view reading as something that takes place between 9:00 and 10:15 every morning or see it as an activity that is pursued only with a basal text. As a result, too many youngsters get the idea that reading is regulated by the clock or by an obscure publisher in a distant city. Too many students view their literacy growth as controlled by external forces.

My philosophy of teaching is that teachers act as facilitators of the learning process rather than monitors. When we sincerely invite youngsters to select and direct their own learning experiences (and teach them to do just that), they can achieve a measure of independence and motivation that will carry them beyond the four walls of the classroom. In short, the way we teach is as important as—if not more important than—what we teach. Indeed, I believe the chief role of a competent educator is to guide students in their own explorations—providing them with the tools they need and the necessary instruction to use those tools and then giving them the chance to discover the joys and excitement of learning as a personal goal rather than a dictated one.

If you have taught for any great length of time, you have undoubtedly experienced the frustration of working with youngsters in "the low group"—trying to provide them with instruction keyed to their needs while juggling the reading demands of other students in the classroom. Or perhaps you're a Title I teacher who is seeking to instill a love of reading in all your students and is constantly looking for materials that will help meet that objective. No matter what your viewpoint, the following suggestions, when used in conjunction with the others in this book, should be helpful in "energizing" the readers under your tutelage.

Give Students Choices

If you are a typical elementary teacher you make approximately 1,500 educational decisions every day. You have to decide everything from who collects the lunch money to when to reschedule the language arts lesson because of the special assembly. Although many of your decisions are small, they must be made nonetheless. I might go so far as to postulate that a major cause of "teacher burnout" is that teachers make too many decisions in the classroom—decisions that rightly belong to students (when they have been trained to make them).

Unfortunately, students have very few opportunities to make decisions that affect their enjoyment and performance. In my experience, students who have opportunities to make choices are more self-assured and competent and take responsibility in the learning process. Following are some specific suggestions.

Allow Students to Select the Books They Want to Read

Further, if the selected book does not hold a child's interest, he or she should be allowed to put it back and select another. My own classroom had nearly 2,500 paperback books organized into three dozen or more categories (sports, mysteries, space exploration, dinosaurs, etc.). By using a series of interest inventories I was able to direct students to those books that best met their needs and interests. It was not necessary or important for them to read every book in the room but rather to have access to a variety of books. Reluctant readers, for example, benefit from easy-to-read books that help them reach a level of fluency.

I have also asked students to rate the books in the classroom by placing a small self-stick dot (available in any stationery store or office supply place) on the back of any book they read. We used five colored dots (red = highly recommended, green = recommended, blue = okay, yellow = bad choice, orange = really rotten). Students could then check the back of each book to see what their fellow students thought of it before making a decision to read it.

Involve Students in Planning and Goal-Setting

Provide opportunities for students to contribute ideas, plans, techniques, and learning possibilities. Do not overrely on teacher's manuals or commercial materials.

Responsible reading occurs when students have opportunities to establish individual goals, monitor those goals, assess those goals, and make decisions on how they can become more actively involved in the reading process. Competent readers do this quite naturally, often without thinking. That may be because they are more internally motivated than the reluctant or remedial readers in a classroom.

Reluctant readers are known by many labels, yet it is important to be aware that their drive or level of motivation is often dependent on what others say or how others react to their reading performance. In short, reluctant readers have a tendency to be "teacher dependent" rather than "student independent." Helping students achieve a level of independence and self-assurance can lead to higher levels of motivation and a more positive self-concept.

Allow Students to Self-Assess

Engaging students in self-assessment procedures fosters independence and enthusiasm for reading. Many of the following strategies can be implemented in a wide variety of classroom activities and can be used for specific individuals as well as small and large groups. Consider using one or more of these frequently.

* Encourage students to evaluate their performance in terms of the goals they set for themselves.

* Have students design some of the questions for any tests or quizzes.

* Design a formal evaluation instrument on a story or book. Instead of having students respond with answers to the questions, ask them to indicate (for each question) whether they: 1) positively know the answer, 2) are mostly sure of the answer, 3) have some idea of the answer, or 4) have no idea what the answer is. Discuss and share reasons (through individual conferences) why students responded as they did.

* Ask students to evaluate the questions in the teacher's edition of the basal text. Encourage them to design a system that rates the queries in terms of difficulty, appropriateness, level of cognition, or any other criterion.

* Encourage students to explain their reasons for selecting answers to specific questions.

* Model your own metacognitive processes as you read aloud to and interact with students.

* Stimulate students to think beyond single right answers. We learn when we are given opportunities to take risks and make mistakes. When children know they have support, they may be encouraged to try new activities or pursue new learning experiences. Students who are stimulated to ask their own questions and are inspired to pursue the answers to those questions achieve high levels of independence in all learning activities.

* When asking questions, suspend judgment and redirect a query to get multiple responses.

* Provide opportunities for students to write down lists of things they learned from a lesson as well as things they did not understand. Take time to discuss those lists and why they did or did not understand.

* Permit students to rate any one of your lessons in terms of *their* level of comprehension. In other words, did your presentation promote understanding and interest? Discuss *your* reactions in terms of *their* perceptions.

* Encourage students to reflect on their errors and what they can do to learn from them.

* Provide a variety of self-correcting assignments within each unit of study.

Provide Recreational Reading

Have poor readers spend lots of time in silent recreational reading and allow them to choose times for this activity. Provide opportunities for them to share and discuss what they read, not to measure their reading progress but rather to offer insights into the nature of reading as a communicative act.

Promote a Whole-Classroom Approach to Reading

Build a community of readers. Don't isolate reluctant readers with labels such as Bluebirds, Eagles, or Iguanas. In short, reduce ability grouping. Reading research demonstrates that in low-ability groups less time is spent on task, less learning occurs, and the quality of teaching is lower than in heterogeneous groups.

Provide sufficient opportunities for readers of different ability levels to interact and share their reading with one another. Mixed-ability groups allow every student to demonstrate competence; they feel a sense of belonging and usefulness. And in cooperative-learning classrooms, academic and affective performance improves for both advantaged and disadvantaged learners.

Build Strong Ties to School and Public Libraries

Librarians have much to contribute to both teachers and students. Work with them to create a revolving classroom collection, foster reading activities, arrange author visits and booktalks, assemble good book lists, manage book discussions and reading award programs, provide one-to-one reading guidance, and offer a host of other services. Librarians can supply teachers with the best read-alouds and the best of each new crop of books.

Make Reading Literature Based

A literature-based reading program has numerous values that set it apart from traditional basal-based or skill-based programs. It promotes reading for meaning, pleasure, and personal development. Flooding your classroom with loads of good books can stimulate the development of positive attitudes as well as positive cognitive growth.

Model Appropriate Reading Behaviors

Teachers who work alongside their students to support and facilitate learning realize they are not repositories of information but models of learning behavior. They promote high-level thinking and deeper examination of concepts that are important to students. They share their enthusiasm for reading with their students. Be "energized" about reading and your students will be, too. In other words, be a student yourself.

Create an Atmosphere of High Expectations

Let underachievers know that you expect high levels of performance from them and will not tolerate shoddy or less-than-adequate work. In other words, make sure your reluctant readers are given the same academic opportunities as are the motivated readers. Are they given equal amounts of time in responding to questions, completing assignments, and participating in reading-related activities?

Meet Students' Needs

"Teaching to the mean"—or providing the same instruction to all students—may be counter productive. Be aware of the learning styles exhibited by all students in your classroom, and provide multilevel activities that encourage students to stretch to the limits of their abilities. Many teachers have discovered that reluctant readers tend to prefer a "hands on," practical approach to learning. They are frustrated when involved in abstract activities (writing essays, determining sequence) and motivated when involved in experiential activities (creating a model, designing a collage).

Emphasize Process over Product, Strategies over Skills

The acts of creation and expression are of greater significance in the development of appropriate language arts skills than are the final products that result from those acts. I do not mean to suggest that products are unimportant, only that when they are deemed of greater significance than the processes that produced them are children less likely to appreciate and learn from all the dynamics of language.

Too often, children perceive learning as a simple accumulation of dozens (perhaps hundreds) of skills. Mastery of a collection of skills is frequently perceived as mastery of a specific subject. In an integrated curriculum, however, the emphasis should be on helping students learn the strategies that will help them in a multitude of learning opportunities. Strategies are more universal than skills and place a premium on use.

Use Whole Texts Rather Than Language Fragments

Exposure to complete stories, books, and poems is important in developing children's reading abilities. Students need to see how all the parts work together. Filling in blank lines on a worksheet or underlining words out of context on a workbook page signals to children that reading is merely the mastery of its *parts* rather than an activity involving appreciation of how those parts work together to create a rich and complete story.

CONNECTION:
Building an Integrated Curriculum

After nearly three decades of teaching experience, I have come to the conclusion that students in literature-rich classrooms demonstrate above-average comprehension as well as strong reading interests. That statement applies equally to average students and to students experiencing reading difficulties. In short, students can reap enormous literary benefits when they are surrounded by literature and provided with activities that have intrinsic meaning for them.

What I am suggesting is that reluctant readers can benefit enormously from an integrated approach to learning. An integrated curriculum has magnificent possibilities for readers who are less than enthusiastic about reading. Here are some ideas for your classroom:

Make Reading Cross-Curricular

Integrate reading into all areas of the curriculum. Try to break away from the idea that reading occurs only during a specific time of day or with specific kinds of books (e.g., textbooks). Design and develop activities in which reading and literature can become an inherent part of every curricular area. Make reading part of the instruction in each subject. In essence, you want to design a broad-based reading program—one that includes all the language arts in all the content areas. Demonstrate the relationships reading has with speaking, writing, and listening and promote those relationships throughout every facet of children's literacy growth.

Integrate the Language Arts Throughout the Curriculum

Children who are provided with active opportunities to participate in the expressive language arts (writing, speaking) also enhance and further develop their appreciation of the interpretive language arts (reading, listening). In short, as students develop higher levels of mastery in one language art, they enhance the development of other language arts as well. The language arts are not separate or divorced from each other. They are intertwined and interrelated and are dependent on each other in facilitating an individual's overall reading development.

Integrate Language and Language Use into Every Curricular Area

The integrated curriculum helps youngsters build bridges and establish connections between subject areas. Learning is seen less as a memorization of disjointed facts and more as an interrelationship of ideas bound by a common "cement"—the language arts. It is through the language arts that children can learn about the world around them and take their place as givers and receivers of worldly information.

Integrate Students' Interests and Needs with Aims of the Curriculum

Children are provided with authentic opportunities to contribute to their own learning through meaningful learning activities. An integrated approach accommodates students of varying abilities and needs and provides learning experiences that are relevant, developmental, and specific. Students can make an "investment of self" in the day-to-day affairs of the classroom and reap the benefits of a personal curriculum.

Engage Students in Real-World Activities

It is doubtful that many students will spend some or all of their lives circling words on a sheet of paper or underlining the verbs on a business document. What they will do is read different types of literature, write letters and manuscripts for others to read, communicate with friends and family members, and listen to news broadcasts and public speakers. The value of an integrated curriculum lies in providing youngsters with the competencies they will need long after they leave your classroom.

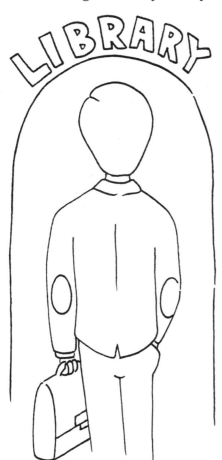

The Integrated Curriculum provides literature-based integrated activities designed to open up learning possibilities for the reluctant readers in your classroom. You should feel free to select, adapt, or modify activities in keeping with the needs and abilities of your students. Also, be sure to provide students with multiple opportunities to select activities and learning opportunities that have meaning for them. In so doing, you will be providing them with a personal stake in their individual literacy development. Obviously, no single activity is appropriate for every student in your room; nor should all students attempt to complete identical activities. There are many interpretations of literature, and children should be allowed to pursue and elaborate activities that will enhance their appreciation of the significance of literature as a viable vehicle for learning.

Book Extensions

The Integrated Curriculum is designed to provide you with a variety of extending activities that offer youngsters opportunities to become actively involved in the dynamics of individual books—empathizing with the characters, visualizing the settings, comprehending the plots and themes, and creatively experiencing the intentions of the author. It is critical to remember that the effective reading program is based on the opportunities children have to make an "investment of self." By that I mean that when students are provided with an arena that allows them to make choices and carry out those choices, reading becomes more personal and enjoyable. When we give children the chance to engage in a process of self-selection we are telling them that they can become active decision makers and "processors" of their own literacy growth.

Following are varied book extensions that can be part of your reading program. They will be most effective when children are given chances to select those that meet their individual needs and interests. In short, they should not be *assigned* but rather they should be *offered*. In so doing, you will help students develop a measure of independence and autonomy within the reading program and eventually within all areas of your classroom curriculum.

Please feel free to alter or modify any of these suggestions in keeping with the dynamics of your own classroom and the individual strengths of your students. Allow children opportunities to alter or elaborate any activity according to their designs or creative responses. These suggestions are written to students instead of to the teacher. You may wish to collect them in a notebook or post them on a wall of the classroom for students to review periodically. You may wish to read selections out loud to younger students.

Auction

Bring in several types of old paperback books that have been stored at home and are no longer being used. Work with other students to scour your neighborhoods for other books that friends or neighbors might donate. Your class may then wish to make arrangements to hold a "book auction" for other students during a lunch period or at the end of the schoolday. Each book can be auctioned for a few cents, with the proceeds donated to the local library for the purchase of new children's books.

Book of the Month

Work with other students to establish some book clubs in the school. These book clubs can meet either before or after school to discuss new books released during the course of the year, make book recommendations to parents for gifts or holiday buying, or even make recommendations to the school librarian for specific purchases.

Buddy-Buddy

You may wish to set up peer reading groups around the school. You and your friends could pair up with students from different rooms to read together or share ideas about specific books or authors. These "minigroups" could be combined into larger groups for periodic book discussions throughout the year.

Coming Attractions

Make a colorful poster at the beginning of each month that "advertises" a specific reading topic, new book releases, or a collection of books by a favorite author. Then display your posters, for example, "Sports Stories" or "Books by Laura Ingalls Wilder," in various locations in the school.

Author(ities)

As a portion of the language arts program, work together in small groups to write, illustrate, and produce your own books. Stories in these books can be group written stories or other types of creative writing. Make plans to include some of these books in the school library (where a special display can be set up). You may wish to donate some of your books to the local public library.

From *The Integrated Curriculum, Second Edition.* © 1998 Anthony D. Fredericks. Teacher Ideas Press. (800) 237-6124.

People in the Street

Interview several people in your neighborhood concerning their reading interests or preferences. You may wish to collect information on occupations of the interviewees, interests and hobbies, or even popular books and materials they read when they were in school. Information on what people remember most about their own reading experiences in school may be a possibility for a project, too.

Puppet Theater

Design and produce a puppet show based on a book you have read. You can perform your show for other classes in the school (perhaps in grades lower than yours) or perhaps videotape it for presentation at a lunch hour or in individual classrooms.

Role Play

With other students create a simple play based on characters and scenes in a favorite book or story. Make arrangements with the local public library to perform your play for an audience of younger readers. You may even wish to consider visiting a children's hospital or local children's agency to schedule productions.

Cover Up

Select several favorite books from the school library or from your own personal library. Create new dust covers for each book. You may wish to make special arrangements with the school librarian to create a special display area.

Picture This

Set up special bulletin boards around the school or within the local community that "advertise" favorite books. You may wish to focus on the most exciting, scariest, or saddest parts of a book in order to get others to read it. These displays should be changed frequently to provide variety and excitement.

Ad Agency

Develop several magazine-type advertisements for favorite books. These advertisements can then be collected into a portfolio that can be distributed or sent around the school or district. Several large advertisement-type posters could be created and submitted to the local library for display on a regular basis.

Party Time

Make arrangements for an all-school or same-grade-level costume party to which everyone comes dressed as their favorite storybook character (teachers too!). You may be able to invite a local book author, schedule book readings, or present dramatizations of popular stories. Prizes may be awarded for those characterizations most in keeping with the themes of the respective books.

Additional Projects

* Select a "reading buddy" and set aside a certain time during the day when the two of you can read to each other.

* Practice reading a primary-level book and read it aloud to a kindergarten class.

* Tape-record a portion of a book so other students can enjoy it.

* Create recordings of related stories.

* Invite your mother, father, or grandparent to read a book so that you can discuss it together.

* Make a time chart of the six most important events in a book.

* Draw an imaginary setting for a book. What types of illustrations would you include in the book that are not there now?

* Make a crossword puzzle using the names, places, and events from a book.

* Write a series of questions that can be attached to a book for others to answer.

* Make a collage of important events in a book. Cut out pictures from old magazines and paste them on a sheet of construction paper.

* Work with some friends in writing a song for a book. Take one of your favorite songs and substitute some of the words in the book.

* Hold an "election" with all your classmates for the favorite book of the month.

* Invent a comic strip using the characters and events in a book.

* Turn part of a book into a series of cartoons.

* Create a political cartoon about a specific event in a book.

* Write a letter of appreciation to the author of a book, telling him or her why you enjoyed it.

* Evaluate several books in the class library. Work with your classmates in setting up some sort of rating system (1–5, high to low, excellent to poor) to gauge each book.

* Read a new book (or part of a book) each day.

* Write a letter to a friend about what you're learning in a book.

* Read several different books on the same topic.

* Read several books by the same author.

* Keep a journal or diary on your impressions of a book as you read it.

* Make a newspaper about a book.

* Create a review from the point of view of a character in a book.

* Write an original adaptation of an event in a book.

* Set up a "reading corner" filled with periodicals, books, and other printed materials concerning the subject of a book.

* Collect recipes the book characters might enjoy and write a cookbook.

* "Publish" an original adaptation of the book.

* Design and write a newspaper article on an important event in a book.

* Locate and read a relevant magazine article about something that happens in the book.

* With some friends, write an original play based on a book.

* Write a poem about something in a book.

* Write a letter to a character or historical figure.

* Write a sequel or prequel to an incident or event in a book.

* Adapt an event in a book into a news report or TV program.

* Create multiple endings for a book.

* Write a description of a book in 25 words or less. In 50 words or less. In 75 words or less.

* Create interview questions for a guest speaker.

* Rewrite a portion of a book with students as major figures.

* Create a glossary or dictionary of important words in a book.

* Create a rebus story for younger students.

* Write riddles about events or circumstances in a book.

* Design a "question box" containing questions and answers about specific books.

* Keep a card file of all the books you've read.

* Print important phrases or quotations from a book on construction paper and post throughout the room.

* Set up a message center to send messages to classmates and the teacher about books you have read.

* Create a calendar or timeline of important events that took place in the story.

* Pretend you're a character in a book and write a letter to someone in your class.

* Write a travel guide or itinerary for someone who wishes to journey to the settings of a book.

* Create a want ad for something in a book. Create job want ads for characters in a book.

* Write a horoscope for a book character.

* Create a scrapbook about important places, people, and events in the book.

* Write a ten-question quiz for the book.

* Create a word bank of words from different parts of the book.

* Write a picture book (or make a wordless picture book) about a significant event from a book.

* Play a game of 20 Questions about a book.

* Conduct a debate or panel discussion on an issue in a book.

* Interview outside "experts" in the local community about some information mentioned in a book.

* Create a new title for a book.

* Make a list of what else you would like to know on the subject of a book you have read.

* Make a story map of a book.

* Design a trivia game on book facts.

* Create a scale model of a particular location in a book.

* Calculate the amount of time between various events in a book.

* Create bar-graph representations of heights or weights of characters.

* Measure distances between places in a book on a map or globe.

* Design an imaginary blueprint of a building or house mentioned in the book.

* Create word problems using distances between settings, sites, or other geographical areas mentioned in a book.

* Ask classmates to rank their favorite characters in a book.

* Study the history of bookmaking.

* Create a budget to travel to a place in the book.

* Set up a trading post for books in the classroom.
* Create flash cards using illustrations from a book.
* Design a pictograph of book events.
* Create a graph or chart to record book data.
* Create a family tree about a book character.
* Identify foods associated with different characters.
* Create an environmental guide to the setting in the book.
* Make a climate map of an area mentioned in the book.
* Write a logbook on the climate of an area in a book.
* Trace the lives of certain characters in a book.
* Create a display of different forms of transportation mentioned in the book.
* List important discoveries noted in a book.

* Build a scale model of a book character(s) using clay or papier mâché.
* Create a montage of different shelters in a book.
* Create a replica of an historical site described in a book.
* Study sanitary methods in various countries mentioned in a book.
* Investigate the history of a particular area in a book.
* Create an animal or plant scrapbook about species mentioned in the book.
* Create a display of different landforms in a book.
* Create a "bill of rights" for book characters.
* Identify ecological concerns about a book's setting.
* Create a chart of weather patterns in different regions mentioned in the book.
* Construct a "self-history" scrapbook.
* Illustrate portions of a book.

---

* Draw illustrations of each character in a book.

* Create a fashion magazine using book characters.

* Put together time capsules for different time periods in a book.

* Establish a "museum" of book artifacts in one corner of the classroom.

* Create a pop-up book about one important event in a book.

* Draw or paint, on the playground, an outline of a country mentioned in the book.

* Make masks of different book characters.

* Create an original slide show on a book.

* Study paintings related to a book.

* Make a papier mâché head of a major character.

* Make a "flip book" about selected events.

* Design an original flannel board.

* Design and create a diorama of a significant scene in a book.

* Create a three-dimensional display of artifacts associated with a story.

* Give a chalktalk about the book.

* Make "movie rolls" using shoeboxes, adding machine tape, and pencils (as the "rollers").

* Locate paintings that relate to scenes mentioned in the book.

* Design a transparency about an important event in a book and show it to the class.

* Create a salt map of a specific location.

* Develop an exercise program for a book figure.

* List the physical skills needed to climb a mountain, conquer a distant land, or navigate an ocean.

* Invent games (for example, Continent Twister).

* Play games from different parts of the world.

* Create a "question-and-answer relay" using specific book facts.

* Create a radio show about a book.

* Act out events in a story and videotape your performances.

* Design costumes for characters in a story.

* Pantomime selected events in a story.

* Create a cultural concert based on a book.

* Sing folk songs associated with a book.

* Role play a confrontation or a scene between book characters.

* Present examples of music associated with various characters or settings.

* Design a filmstrip for a book (special filmstrip kits can be obtained from education dealers).

* Give dramatic readings of a book.

* Select and include appropriate musical selections for an oral reading of the book.

* Set up an auction of items belonging to various book characters.

* Write your reaction to a book on an index card and file it in a recipe box. Encourage others to do the same.

* Make up several newspaper headlines about book events.

* List the qualities you like in a friend. Which book character comes closest to those qualities?

* Create a wanted poster for one or more book characters.

* Cut silhouettes of book characters from construction paper and retell the story to a small group of classmates.

* Explain which book character you would like to have as a next-door neighbor.

* Write to a pen pal in another classroom explaining what you like most and least about the book.

* Look in the telephone book for the names of people similar to the names of book characters.

* Work with some classmates to develop and design a "who's who" of selected book characters.

* Set up a "literary review panel" of classmates who can read and recommend books to other students based on their interests, free-time activities, or hobbies.

* Set up a TV news team to report on book events as they happen.

* Establish an "academy awards" for books judged to have the best characters, most colorful illustrations, or best design (for example).

* Take on the role of a book character and write an autobiography.

* Write a movie script for a favorite book.

PARTICIPATORY COMPREHENSION:
Processes (Not Panaceas) for Reluctant Readers

The concept of participatory comprehension underscores and emphasizes the reader's purposeful involvement in textual material. Readers who are provided with multiple opportunities to control, direct, and monitor their comprehension growth develop strategies that facilitate understanding and stimulate enjoyment.

In contrast to learning based on externally generated controls that "guide" passive readers through a maze of artificially contrived demands, participatory comprehension focuses on the reader, not the text. The reader actively manipulates text rather than the other way around. Readers generate expectations and questions based on prior knowledge and the evolving meaning of a text. They process information, develop inferences, activate appropriate concepts, and relate new information to old. Participatory comprehension thus stimulates a sense of ownership, or what I prefer to call "an investment of self," in the reading act.

To foster a participatory approach to comprehension development and a rise in the number of "energized" readers as opposed to reluctant readers, teachers need effective strategies. Following are several you can incorporate into your reading lessons to promote an active engagement in the reading process. Obviously, you will not want to use these approaches with every book that each student reads. Youngsters need opportunities to meld their reading experiences with the experiences of other subject areas; they also need many opportunities to read simply for the sake of enjoyment.

Student-Generated Questions

When students begin asking questions about what they are reading, they are beginning to assume one of the major roles of an accomplished, active reader. Giving students an opportunity to generate questions that have meaning for them is a powerful incentive to pursue answers in text. You and I do this quite naturally when we read the daily newspaper. For example, if we were to see a headline that said "Government to Raise Taxes 20%," we might ask ourselves questions such as "How will this affect my family?" "Will I need to get a second job?" or "When will this take place?" We would then begin reading that article to find the answers to the questions we had generated. In other words, we are motivated to read that article because we have a personal stake in the information it contains.

When you provide reluctant readers in your classroom with similar opportunities to generate questions about text and pursue the answers, you give them a forum in which they can develop a level of intrinsic motivation and interact with the entire reading process. The following questioning strategy—the student motivated active reading technique (SMART)—is a comprehension strategy that provides students with opportunities to become personally involved in both expository and narrative reading. Self-initiated questions and concept development underscore the utility of SMART in a wide range of reading situations and abilities.

SMART is appropriate for individuals as well as small and large groups and can be organized as follows:

1. A book, story, or reading selection is chosen (by the teacher) for the group or individual to discuss. Paper and pencils are provided to record questions and thoughts.

2. The teacher writes the title of the book on the chalkboard and encourages the group members or the individual to ask questions about the title of the selection. The teacher records all questions.

3. The individual or group makes predictions about the content of the selection. The student(s) decides which questions are most appropriate for exploration and ranks them accordingly.

4. Students examine illustrations found in the book or story and propose questions. The initial prediction(s) is modified or altered according to information shared on the illustrations.

5. The individual or group reads the selection (either orally or silently), looking for answers to the recorded questions. Also, students may generate new questions for discussion. As they find answers in the text, they talk about them and attempt to arrive at mutually satisfying responses.

6. The procedure continues throughout the remainder of the selection: Students seek answers to previously generated questions and continue to ask additional questions. Upon completion of the book, they discuss all recorded questions and answers. The individual or group decides on all appropriate answers. Students are encouraged to refer back to the book to answer any lingering questions.

7. The individual or group can participate in one or more follow-up activities:

   a. Write or tell a new ending.
   b. Would another title be more appropriate?
   c. How would the story be different if ...?
   d. What would happen if ...?

8. More often than not a bank of unanswered student-generated questions will remain (my students and I found that we could locate between 60 and 80 percent of the answers in most stories). Many of the answers can be pursued in other resources such as supplemental trade books, encyclopedias, and reference sources. Any questions still remaining can be discussed in terms of their appropriateness to the book, their level of cognition, or the need to restructure or even eliminate them as inappropriate.

Keep in mind three essential points as you use SMART with your students. First, students may be reluctant to use this process for the first two or three weeks. This is simply because they have not been provided with previous opportunities to ask their own questions—they have become too "teacher dependent." If it is true that teacher talk takes up about 80 percent of classroom time, it should also be evident that individual students do not have a lot of opportunities to engage in oral discourse, much less ask their own questions.

Second, students will tend to ask the kinds of questions they are asked in class. If you spend a great deal of time asking low-level, literal, or factual questions, students follow this model. If you consistently model high-level, creative, and imaginative questions, students will again tend to follow your lead. In fact, it is possible to get a sense of the level of thinking in a classroom by providing students with a chance to ask their own questions.

Third and key to the success of SMART, the teacher slowly begins to take a passive role in the process; that is, you need to assist students in assuming responsibility for initiating and answering their own questions. Guiding students toward higher levels of thinking is a major goal of this strategy.

MM&M
(Metacognitive Modeling and Monitoring)

One truism remains constant whenever we talk about reading: We can never see what is going on in the mind of a reader as he or she reads a piece of text. In other words, although we can use several forms of external diagnosis to differentiate the good readers from the poor readers, we are never completely sure of the strategies any reader uses (or chooses not to use).

MM&M provides reluctant readers with an opportunity to "see" inside the mind of good readers as they go through the reading process. In essence, the teacher serves as a model of efficient reading, demonstrating for students the thought processes and mental activities used while reading. When struggling readers are made aware of the strategies good readers use (inside their heads), they can emulate those strategies.

In this strategy you select reading material and begin to "think out loud," verbalizing about your thinking as you read. Initially, you will want to select a piece of textual material that is short and contains some obvious points of difficulty (vocabulary, sequence of events, ambiguities, etc.). Read this passage aloud to students, stopping at selected points and verbalizing the thought processes you are using to work through any difficulties. This verbalization is essential in that it provides a viable model for students to "copy" whenever they run into comprehension difficulties in their reading. Here are examples of the five steps:

1. Make predictions (demonstrate the importance of making hypotheses).

    "From this title, I predict that this story will be about a missing ring and a haunted house."

    "In the next chapter, I think we'll find out how the two twins were able to sail to the other side of the lake."

    "I think this next part will describe what the thief took from the dresser drawer."

2. Describe your mental images (show how mental pictures are formed in your head as you read).

> "I can see a picture of an old man walking down a country lane with his dog at his side."

> "I'm getting a picture in my mind of a sparsely furnished apartment with very small rooms."

> "The picture I have in my mind is that of a very short girl with curly red hair and a face full of freckles."

3. Share an analogy (show how the information in the text may be related to something in one's background knowledge).

> "This is like the time I had to take my daughter to the hospital in the middle of the night."

> "This is similar to the time I first learned to ski in Colorado and kept falling down."

> "This seems to be like the day we had to take our family dog to the vet to be put to sleep."

4. Verbalize a confusing point (show how you keep track of your level of comprehension as you read).

> "I'm not sure what is happening here."

> "This is turning out a little differently than I expected."

> "I guess I was correct in my original prediction."

5. Demonstrate "fix-up" strategies (let students see how you repair any comprehension problems).

> "I think I need to reread this part of the story."

> "Maybe this word is explained later in the story."

> "Now that part about the fishing rod makes sense to me."

These five steps can and should be modeled for students in several different kinds of reading material. As you read and model, allow students opportunities to verbalize thoughts. Your goal, obviously, is to have students internalize these processes so that they can use them independently with all kinds of reading material. Here are some alternate approaches to MM&M:

1. Have students practice the procedure with a partner. One student reads a passage out loud to another and verbalizes some of his or her thinking. The partner records those thought processes and discusses them with the reader upon completion of the story.

2. Students can read a passage into a tape recorder. Afterward, they can play the recording and stop at selected points and tell a partner or you about some of their thinking as they dealt with the text at that spot.

3. Bring in other adults to the classroom to model their thinking behavior as they read. The principal, secretary, custodian, librarian, superintendent, and other school-related personnel can all be positive reading models for students. Be sure to provide a brief "in-service" on MM&M for each reader prior to the presentation.

4. Invite students from grades higher than yours to visit the classroom and read selected passages to your students. Ask them to model their thinking as they read.

5. Designate a student "reader of the day" who selects a passage to share with other students and demonstrates the MM&M procedure. This daily event validates every student as a model for all the other students and the utility of this strategy for all readers in all types of material.

Prediction Cards

Prediction cards allow students to tap into their background knowledge about the topic of a book, share that information with classmates, and make predictions about the content of a piece of literature. At the same time, students can manipulate their vocabulary and share ideas related to word study and comprehension of text. Although this strategy works particularly well with nonfiction materials, it can also be used with narrative text.

1. Before students read a book, select 20–25 words from throughout the book. Include words you know students are familiar with, words essential to comprehension of text, and a few unknown words.

2. Print the words on index cards and distribute the cards to a small group of students. (You can make multiple sets for multiple groups of students.)

3. Invite students to assemble the cards into categories of their own choosing (NOTE: Do not tell them a specific number of categories or the number of "word cards" that should be in each category). Encourage students to place words in categories according to their own knowledge of those words or their predictions of how those words might be used in the forthcoming text.

4. Invite student groups to share their various categories and provide rationales for the placement of word cards within specific groups.

5. Invite students to read the text looking for the words on the index cards. After the reading, encourage students to rearrange the cards or manipulate the words into new categories or groupings based on the information gleaned from the text. Afterward, invite students to discuss reasons for any rearrangements and compare their placements with those of other groups.

As part of the unit African People and Their Culture, Derek Alden and his students wanted to investigate some of the flora and fauna of different regions of the African continent. Derek introduced his students to a wide range of literature describing the animal and plant life of Africa. One of the books he used was *Hippo* by Caroline Arnold (New York: Mulberry Books, 1989; this book describes the life and habits of hippos—those that live in captivity as well as the various species that live throughout Africa). In preparation for their study of the book, Derek prepared several sets of prediction cards. He selected words from throughout the book, including words known by his students and vocabulary important to their overall comprehension. The words illustrated in Figure 1.1 below are those Derek used with his students.

Figure 1.1. Sample Prediction Cards.

enclosure	banks	mammals	youngster	territory
pygmy	enormous	underwater	enemies	herd
newborn	appetite	submerged	nostril	preserves
bristles	kilograms	alfalfa	vegetarian	molars
dung	nutrients	incisors	captivity	exhibit

Derek made five complete sets of these 25 words. He presented each of five groups of students with a set of prediction cards and invited them to arrange their cards in categories of their own choosing. Afterward, he invited the groups to share their categories with the entire class. Discussion centered on some of the differences among the categories and the various types of background information shared within the groups of students.

Later, Derek read the book to his students, inviting them to listen for the words on the prediction cards. Upon finishing the book, Derek asked his students to rearrange the cards according to the information they learned in the book. As before, students worked in groups, sharing and comparing data and facts learned from the book. Students were encouraged to discuss any differences between the arrangement of cards before the reading of the book and new arrangements made after hearing Derek read the book aloud. Students were amazed to discover the ways in which their background information could be combined with the book information to create a host of new categories.

From *The Integrated Curriculum, Second Edition.* © 1998 Anthony D. Fredericks. Teacher Ideas Press. (800) 237-6124.

K-W-L

K-W-L (Ogle, 1986) is a three-step framework that helps students access appropriate information in expository writing. It takes advantage of students' background knowledge and helps demonstrate relationships between that knowledge and the information in the text.

K-W-L (what I **K**now, what I **W**ant to learn, what I **L**earned) involves students in three major cognitive steps—accessing their background knowledge about a topic, determining what they would like to learn about that subject, and evaluating what was learned about the topic. Figure 1.2 presents a paradigm through which teachers and students can begin to read expository text. The following steps can be used (each number is keyed to the figure):

1. Invite students to talk about what they already know about the topic of the text. This information should be freely volunteered and written on the chalkboard or in the first section (K—What we know) of the chart (which can be duplicated and given to the class).

2. Encourage students to categorize the information they have volunteered. They can do this through various grouping strategies such as semantic webbing. These groupings can be recorded in section 2 on the chart.

3. Invite students to make predictions about the types of information the text will contain. These predictions should be based on their background knowledge and the categories of information elicited in step 2.

4. Encourage students to generate their own questions about the text. These can be discussed and recorded in the "W—What we want to find out" section of the chart.

5. Invite students to read the text and record any answers to their questions. Students may wish to do this individually or in small groups.

6. Upon completion of the text provide students with an opportunity to discuss the information learned and how it relates to their prior knowledge. Talk about questions posed for which no information was found in the text. Help students discover other sources for finding the answers.

Figure 1.2. K-W-L Strategy Sheet.

1. K—What we know	4. W—What we want to find out	6. L—What we learned & still need to learn

2. *Categories of information we expect to use:*

    A.   E.

    B.   F.

    C.   G.

    D.   H.

3. *Predictions on the information included in the text:*

    A.

    B.

    C.

    D.

5. *Answers to self-initiated questions discovered in the text:*

SOURCE: Adapted from Ogle, D. "K-W-L: A Teaching Model That Develops Active Reading of Expository Text," *The Reading Teacher*, February 1986, pp. 564–70.

From *The Integrated Curriculum, Second Edition.* © 1998 Anthony D. Fredericks. Teacher Ideas Press. (800) 237-6124.

Anticipation Guide

Anticipation guides alert students to some of the major concepts in textual material before it is read. Thus, students have an opportunity to share ideas and opinions as well as activate their prior knowledge about a topic before they read about it. It is also a helpful technique for eliciting students' misconceptions about a subject. Students become actively involved in the dynamics of reading a specified selection because they have an opportunity to talk about the topic before reading about it.

1. Read the story or selection and attempt to select the major concepts, ideas, or facts in the text. For example, in a selection on weather the following might be determined:

   a. There are many different types of clouds.
   b. Examples of severe weather include tornadoes, hurricanes, and thunderstorms.
   c. Precipitation occurs in the form of rain, snow, sleet, and hailstones.
   d. Many types of weather occur along "fronts."

2. Create five to ten statements (not questions) that reflect common misconceptions about the subject, are ambiguous, or are indicative of students' prior knowledge. Statements can be written on the chalkboard or photocopied and distributed. (Using the previous observations about weather, the statements indicated in figure 1.3 might result.)

3. Give students plenty of opportunities to agree or disagree with each statement. Whole-class or small group discussions would be appropriate. After discussions, ask each student to record a positive or negative response to each statement. Initiate discussions focusing on reasons for individual responses.

4. Direct students to read the text, keeping in mind the statements and their individual or group reactions to those statements.

5. After students have read the selection, engage the class in a discussion on how the textual information may have changed their opinions. Provide students with an opportunity to record their reactions to each statement based on what they read in the text. It is not important that a consensus be reached or that the students agree with everything the author states. The emphasis is on students engaging in an active dialogue that allows them to react to the relationships between prior knowledge and current knowledge.

In Michelle Epsom's unit on oceanography, students expressed an interest in the weather patterns that form over the oceans and the effect those weather patterns have on various land areas. The effects of a recent hurricane that had destroyed areas of Florida had received front-page coverage in the *Los Angeles Times* and sparked students' curiosity about how hurricanes form over the Atlantic Ocean. Based on her students' interests, Michelle introduced her class to the book *Weather Forecasting* by Gail Gibbons (New York: Aladdin Books, 1993). In preparation for their study of the book, Michelle prepared the anticipation guide in figure 1.3.

Figure 1.3. Sample Anticipation Guide for Weather.

DIRECTIONS: Look at the sentences on this page. The statements are numbered from 1 to 6. Read each sentence; if you think that what it says is correct, print "*Yes*" on the line under the word "BEFORE." If you think the sentence is wrong, print "*No*" on the line under the word "BEFORE." Do the same thing for each sentence. Remember how to do this because you will do it again *after* you read the selection.

BEFORE   AFTER

_____   _____   1.   Hurricanes are the most destructive form of weather.

_____   _____   2.   Precipitation is any type of moisture that falls from clouds.

_____   _____   3.   Thunderstorms occur when a cold front meets and rises over a warm front.

_____   _____   4.   There are five basic types of clouds.

_____   _____   5.   Fog can be defined as a cloud on the ground.

_____   _____   6.   Typhoons occur in the Pacific Ocean.

Working as a class, students responded to each of the statements on the anticipation guide. Class discussion centered on reasons for their choices and predictions about what they might discover in the forthcoming book. Michelle then provided multiple copies of the book to students and invited them to read and locate confirming data related to each of the identified statements. Afterward, students completed the "AFTER" column of the guide and shared their reasons for placing "Yes" or "No" on each line. Follow-up discussions revealed some differences of opinion, yet the conversation was lively as well as supportive. Students found that they each brought different perspectives to a book and could all benefit from those differences in a mutually stimulating learning environment.

Anticipation guides are also appropriate for use with fiction material. Figure 1.4 (p. 26) shows an anticipation guide for the book *The Salamander Room* by Anne Mazer (New York: Knopf, 1991) that could be used as part of a unit on animals or ecology.

Figure 1.4. Sample Anticipation Guide for *The Salamander Room*.

DIRECTIONS: Look at the sentences on this page. The statements are numbered from 1 to 5. Read each sentence; if you think that what it says is correct, print "*Yes*" on the line under the word "BEFORE." If you think the sentence is wrong, print "*No*" on the line under the word "BEFORE." Do the same thing for each sentence. Remember how to do this because you will do it again *after* you read the book *The Salamander Room*.

<u>**BEFORE**</u>   <u>**AFTER**</u>

_____   _____   1.   Salamanders live under dried leaves.

_____   _____   2.   Most salamanders are orange in color.

_____   _____   3.   Salamanders eat crickets and other insects for food.

_____   _____   4.   The diet of salamanders is similar to the diet of frogs.

_____   _____   5.   Salamanders are an important part of the ecology of the forest.

_____   _____   6.   People should not remove animals from their natural habitat.

Reflective Sharing Technique

The reflective sharing technique demonstrates the interrelationships that naturally exist between the language arts and specific curricular areas. This strategy stimulates children to use language as a basis for learning across the curriculum. The reflective sharing technique encourages students to share and discuss ideas that are important to them while reacting in positive ways to each other.

1.   Choose a book or story appropriate to the interests of your students or their developing reading abilities. Determine the general subject area of the story and record it on the chalkboard.

2.   For approximately three to five minutes invite students to brainstorm for as many ideas, concepts, or items that could be included in that subject area. These items can be recorded on the chalkboard. Brainstorming should stimulate a free flow of ideas irrespective of their quality. The emphasis should be on generating a quantity of ideas and a wide range of responses.

3.   Ask each student to select one of the ideas from the list on the board. Invite each student to write about his or her selected item for about five minutes (this time limit can be adjusted according to the age or ability levels of students).

From *The Integrated Curriculum, Second Edition.* © 1998 Anthony D. Fredericks. Teacher Ideas Press. (800) 237-6124.

4. Sharing what each person has composed is the most important part of this activity.

    a. Divide students into groups of four (it is important to have groups of four for the sharing process, but if this is not possible, eliminate roles 3 and 4 in the following when necessary). In each group of four, members take specific roles:

        Person 1 reads what he or she wrote.

        Person 2 summarizes what Person 1 read.

        Person 3 tells what he or she liked about what Person 1 read.

        Person 4 tells something else he or she would like to know about the subject about which Person 1 wrote.

    b. After one round of sharing, the process is repeated until four rounds are completed and each student has taken on all four roles.

Figure 1.5. Reflective Sharing Technique.

ROLE	Round 1	Round 2	Round 3	Round 4
Reads what he or she wrote	Person 1	Person 2	Person 3	Person 4
Summarizes reader's story	Person 2	Person 3	Person 4	Person 1
Tells what he or she liked	Person 3	Person 4	Person 1	Person 2
Tells something else he or she wants to know	Person 4	Person 1	Person 2	Person 3

5. Provide the groups with an opportunity to share some of the ideas discussed in their sessions(s) with the entire class (it is not necessary to have every group share, because some ideas will be redundant). Point out to students the wealth of information they already have about the subject of the book or story even before they begin to read it. You may wish to invite students to discuss how their past experience reflects ideas in the book.

6. At this point you may wish to invite students to read the book independently or share the book with them orally. (NOTE: With younger students you may wish to conduct the reflective sharing technique as an oral activity. Select students to talk about special interests. The entire class summarizes, reacts, and asks questions for further exploration.)

Character Continuum

The character continuum is a delightful postreading strategy that helps students discuss information related to the qualities of selected characters in a story. With some minor modifications (see fig. 1.6), this strategy can also be used to help students focus on the setting of a story.

1. Ask students to brainstorm for all the words they can think of that can be used to describe one or more characters in a story. Write all the words on the chalkboard or overhead projector.

2. Invite students to suggest antonyms for most or all of the recorded words.

3. Place each word pair at opposite ends of a continuum (see fig. 1.6). For primary-level youngsters six to eight lines are sufficient; for intermediate students eight to twelve lines are adequate.

4. Invite students to work in pairs, small groups, or as a whole class to place an X on each line indicating the degree to which an identified character exhibits a particular trait (there are no right or wrong answers).

5. Encourage students to discuss their rationale for placement of the X's. Rereading of portions of the book may be necessary to verify information or assumptions.

6. Students may wish to create a master continuum that can be duplicated and used repeatedly with other characters in other stories. Separate continuums can also be developed for story settings.

Figure 1.6. Sample Character Continuum.

Book Title: _____

Character: _____

Friendly. . . . . Unfriendly

Happy. . . . . Sad

Popular . . . . Unpopular

Wise. . . . . Foolish

Outgoing . . . . Shy

Unselfish . . . . Selfish

Sociable . . . . Unsociable

Ambitious . . . . Lazy

Neat. . . . . Messy

Honest . . . . Dishonest

Brave . . . . Cowardly

Kind. . . . . Cruel

The character continuum above can be used "as is" or as a prototype for those created by you and your students.

Figure 1.7 is a character continuum that Brenda Youngston's students created for the book *Why the Sun and the Moon Live in the Sky* by Elphinstone Dayrell (Boston: Houghton Mifflin, 1968; this is an African folktale that explains how the sun and the moon came to live in the sky). One of the major characters is the sun; the following continuum was created after Brenda had read the first half of the book to the class.

Figure 1.7. Character Continuum for
Why the Sun and the Moon Live in the Sky.

Book Title: _____*Why the Sun and the Moon Live in the Sky*_____

Character: _____The Sun_____

Friendly . X . . . . Unfriendly

Happy . X . . . . Sad

Popular . . . . X . . . . Unpopular

Wise . . . . .X . . . . . Foolish

Outgoing . . . . X . . . . Shy

Unselfish . X . . . . Selfish

Sociable . . . X . . . . Unsociable

Ambitious . . . . X . . . . Lazy

Neat . . . . .X . . . . Messy

Honest . X . . . . Dishonest

Brave . . . . .X. . . . . Cowardly

Kind . . X . . . . Cruel

After students had completed the character continuum, Brenda read the rest of the book to them. She then invited them to consider repositioning any of their X's on the continuum lines as a result of hearing the second half of the story. In this way, Brenda helped her students understand how characters develop throughout a story.

Figure 1.8 (p. 32) is an example of a setting continuum that can be used with students. The words and their antonyms have all been suggested by students in a second-grade classroom. You are encouraged to invite your students to suggest their own words (and their antonyms) for continuums used in your classroom.

Figure 1.8. Sample Setting Continuum.

Book Title: _____

Setting: _____

Hot · Cold

Urban · Rural

Friendly · Hostile

Flat · Hilly

Near Ocean · Far from Ocean

Colorful · Plain

New · Old

Setting continuums (just like character continuums) can be used with a variety of narrative materials. The best ones, however, will be those developed by the entire class or small groups of students.

A modification of the character continuum is the facts/attitude continuum, which is appropriate for use with nonfiction material. The procedure is similar to that previously outlined, except that students are encouraged to suggest facts about a topic as well as their attitudes or perceptions about it. These items (and their accompanying antonyms) are arranged on continuum lines as before. Students are invited to complete these after reading a book. (NOTE: This exercise is also appropriate as a prereading strategy, with students suggesting ideas based on their background knowledge of a forthcoming topic.)

Figure 1.9 is an example of a facts/attitude continuum created by Tracy Palmer and her students in preparation for the book *Animals at the Water's Edge* by Charles P. Milne (Minneapolis: Raintree, 1988).

Figure 1.9. Facts/Attitude Continuum for *Animals at the Water's Edge*.

Book Title: ___Animals at the Water's Edge___

Topic: ___Mussels___

Author: ___Charles P. Milne___

Publisher: ___Raintree, 1988___

Strong . X . . . . Weak

Neat . . . . .X . . Yucky

Useful . . . . X. . . . . Harmful

Eat Meat . . . . X . . . . Eat Plants

Important . . . . .X . . . . Worthless

Live Birth . . . . X . . . . Eggs

Not Poisonous . X . . . . Poisonous

Fun . . . . X . . . . Boring

Industrious . . . . X . . Lazy

Underground . . . . X . Above Ground

All of the participatory comprehension strategies presented in this section stimulate reluctant readers and enhance their reading experiences. They provide you with multiple opportunities to help students become active participants in the reading process and motivated learners throughout all dimensions of the elementary curriculum.

USING CHILDREN'S LITERATURE ACROSS THE CURRICULUM

Children who have many opportunities to examine and explore all types of literature, particularly in a supportive and interactive environment, develop a lifelong appreciation for books and stories. And when children are given a chance to integrate literature into each and every aspect of their lives, they begin to understand its importance as a conduit of knowledge, wonder, and imagination. Making literature a part of every aspect of the elementary curriculum is a primary goal of this book. In reaching this goal, the following concepts are key:

1. *Interactive processes.* Children provided with opportunities to interact with and actively extend appropriate books sense the dynamics of literature across the curriculum.

2. *Active participation.* Too often, children are exposed to literature in a passive context. The approach in this book is grounded in the belief that students can elaborate, extend, and expand the concepts of a single book throughout their daily curriculum.

3. *Strategic comprehension.* Providing learners with a chance to develop their own purposes for reading and to reflect on those purposes is at the heart of any successful reading campaign. This book recognizes that youngsters have the capacity for developing individual techniques necessary to effectively tackle a learning task and that they can modify or adjust their perceptions throughout that process.

4. *Motivation.* Stimulating youngsters to engage in learning tasks and maintain a high level of motivation continues to be a major concern of many teachers. This book is designed to foster an interest in all learning skills such that performance and persistence are maintained in a variety of positive academic situations. Young learners develop positive attitudes about their abilities as well as about the materials they are using.

5. *Divergent thinking.* Students who are provided unlimited opportunities to both process and interpret information are those who succeed in any learning activity. The activities in this book offer children many ways to move beyond the "right answer" into new areas of thinking and cognition. Students are engaged in a rich and enthusiastic learning environment that does not limit their possibilities but rather enhances them.

This book is a discovery approach to literature. When students are provided with opportunities to examine, process, and utilize literature in subjects such as reading/language arts, science/health, art, math, music, social studies, and physical education, their growth as learners mushrooms accordingly.

"Bookwebbing" is a process that extends literature across the curriculum. It offers students a multitude of opportunities to make connections among subjects, to extend and expand their learning into a variety of topics, and to promote reading as a universal "subject."

The focal point of bookwebbing is a single piece of literature. From that book a variety of activities and projects can emanate—each related to a particular area of the curriculum. It is important that students have opportunities to participate in creating and designing these activities in keeping with their interests and needs. The following steps apply to designing bookwebbing activities for any literature selection.

1. Select a book most students have read.

2. List the title of the book in the center of the chalkboard.

3. Discuss with students some of the events, characters, or settings from the book.

4. List the names of other curricular subjects on the sides of the chalkboard (see fig. 2.1).

5. Have students brainstorm for related activities within each curricular area, each of which could be used to extend and enhance the book. Students can work in small groups—each group "assigned" one of the subjects of the curriculum—and generate an extensive list of possible projects.

6. Initially, you will want students to generate a *quantity* of ideas; later you can emphasize *quality* ideas.

7. After the master list has been created, provide students with an opportunity to select one or more of the listed activities and use them.

Here's a diagram of a bookweb that needs to be filled in:

Figure 2.1. Sample Bookweb.

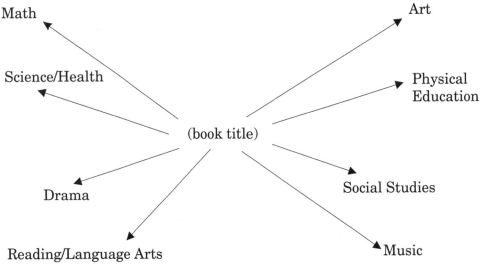

As students engage in their self-selected activities, be sure to provide them with opportunities to refer to the book and draw relationships between the projects they are engaged in and the ideas, themes, or concepts presented in the literature selection. In this way, you will be ensuring that students understand the interrelationships that exist between literature and the other subject areas.

Following is an example of how one book—*Dear Mr. Henshaw* by Beverly Cleary—was developed into a multidisciplinary unit using the bookwebbing strategy.

Math

1. Have students count the number of butterflies in a given area over a certain period of time.

2. Students can collect data on the size, dimensions, and weight of different types of trucks.

3. Have students calculate the number of letters Leigh Botts sent to Mr. Henshaw.

Science/Health

1. Have students construct their own form of burglar alarm from wires, batteries, and bells.

2. Investigate the life cycle of butterflies.

3. Have students learn about engines and the nature of force, power, and movement.

Drama

1. Have students create a skit about a day in the life of a book writer.

2. Have students write a play about an imaginary truck driver.

3. Students may wish to create a puppet show using some of the characters in the book.

Art

1. Students can make a collage of trucks, semis, and tractor trailers.

2. Have students make a book in the shape of a butterfly and create their own "butterfly" story.

3. Have students draw an illustration of the saddest part of the story.

Physical Education

1. Design an obstacle course on the playground that simulates the route the butterflies take to and from Pacific Grove.

2. Have students invent conditioning exercises for truck drivers.

3. Have students discuss how animals (dogs) can stay in shape.

Social Studies

1. Have students look into the history of book publishing.

2. Have students look into some of the costs involved in truck driving or catering.

3. Have students look into all the states mentioned in the book.

Reading/Language Arts

1. Have students prepare an invitation for an author, truck driver, or caterer to visit the classroom.

2. Have students create a quiz show on letter-writing procedures.

3. Encourage students to establish a pen pal program with another classroom.

Music

1. Play Saint-Saëns's *Carnival of the Animals* and direct students to imagine what instrument(s) would duplicate the sound of butterflies.

2. Ask students to choose some popular children's songs and rewrite the lyrics using facts from the story.

3. Have students select music they think Leigh would enjoy. Ask them to defend their choices.

In my experience, reluctant readers enthusiastically embrace bookwebbing and it becomes a powerful motivational force in their academic pursuits. In fact, I have discovered that there is no end to the possibilities that can be designed for any single book.

GRADE 2

Bugs

Nancy Winslow Parker and Joan Richards Wright
New York: Mulberry, 1987

Summary

A fascinating examination of 15 common insects, this book is a creative look into the world of these tiny creatures. Rich and colorful illustrations and a mix of fiction and nonfiction make this an engaging text.

Critical Thinking Questions

1. Of all the bugs mentioned in the book, which one was your favorite? Why?

2. How many of the bugs described in the book have you seen around your house or neighborhood? Which one frightens you the most?

3. Why do you think some people are afraid of bugs? Why do people try to get rid of bugs from their homes?

Reading/Language Arts

1. Here are some other books about bugs that students may enjoy reading: *Fireflies* by J. Brinckloe (New York: Macmillan, 1985); *Insects Do the Strangest Things* by L. Hornblow and A. Hornblow (New York: Random House, 1989); *Ants* by Angel Julivert (Hauppauge, NY: Barron's, 1991); *Insects That Live in Families* by D. Morris (Milwaukee, WI: Raintree, 1987); and *The Golden Book of Insects and Spiders* by Laurence Pringle (Racine, WI: Western, 1990).

2. Invite students to write as a class to *Ranger Rick's Nature Magazine* or *Your Big Backyard* (National Wildlife Federation, 1412 16th St., NW, Washington, DC 20036), asking for information about insects and spiders. Students may be able to obtain free or inexpensive pictures and books that can be displayed and used in the classroom.

3. As a class, brainstorm about what the planet Earth would be like if there were no insects. For example, imagine no more mosquito bites or bee stings, no more honey, no more flowers, no more butterflies, and so on. Invite students to list the positive and negative effects of insects on the chalkboard. They can also write and illustrate stories about the planet with no insects.

Science/Health

1. After students have read the book, ask them to create a make-believe insect that is yet to be discovered. The make-believe insect should be illustrated, named, and a few sentences should be written telling where the insect lives, what it eats, whether it is helpful or a pest, and so on.

2. Obtain a medium-sized, wide-mouth jar that you can cover with a piece of netting or nylon stocking held in place with a rubber band. Then, take a nature walk outside to look for insects. The jar can become the habitat for an insect that students find. Once an insect is caught, be sure to put a twig, leaves, and other materials appropriate for that insect's environment in the jar before covering it. Invite students to observe the insect for a few days, record their findings, and then return it to its original environment.

Art

1. Provide inked stamp pads and invite students to use their thumbprints to make insect/spider bodies and then draw legs and antennae. Encourage students to also illustrate the environment in which they would find their selected creatures.

2. Provide students with an assortment of magazines that contain pictures of insects and spiders. Encourage them to bring in old magazines from home. Invite students to make a class collage by pasting pictures of different insects and spiders on an insect graffiti wall.

Math

1. Invite students to keep a logbook of the numbers of selected bugs located in a specific area (a room in their house, a section of the classroom, a plot of land in the backyard). Encourage students to record numbers of bugs observed during a designated part of each day (from 3:30 to 4:00 P.M., for example) over a selected period of time (one week, for example). Invite students to create a chart or graph that records those numbers and that can be displayed.

Music

1. Several recorded tapes of outdoor and nature sounds are available (one good source is NorthSound, P.O. Box 1360, Minocqua, WI 54548 [1-800-336-6398]). Play one or more of these tapes for students and invite them to identify the objects or animals making those sounds. How many of the animals are insects? What information about those animals can students locate in the school library?

Social Studies

1. Many insects live in social groups. Ants and termites, mentioned in the book, are two examples of social insects. Share the book *Ant Cities* by Arthur Dorros (New York: Harper and Row, 1987) and discuss with students the similarities between ant cities and the cities that people live in. What are the related elements of those two types of cities? What elements of one type of city are missing from the other type of city? (NOTE: Directions for the creation of an ant farm are included in the book *Ant Cities*. Students may wish to create their own ant city and observe the social behavior of ants firsthand.)

Physical Education

1. Invite students to each select one of the insects mentioned in the book (or another bug of their own choosing). Invite each child to demonstrate the movement of that insect in a designated area. For example, for a mosquito, students can extend their arms and "buzz" around the room; for a centipede, students can wriggle across the room; for a cricket, students can leap on their hands and knees. Provide opportunities for students to describe their movements and why they may be unique to each selected insect.

Frog and Toad Are Friends
Arnold Lobel
New York: Harper and Row, 1970

Summary

This is a collection of five short stories about two friends—a frog and a toad. One story deals with the coming of spring, another is about a special event, and a third is about a missing button. Two other stories concern a funny bathing suit and an important letter.

Critical Thinking Questions

1. Why do you think Frog and Toad are such good friends?

2. What does the word *friendship* mean to you?

3. What are some of the special things friends do for each other?

4. Which of the five stories did you enjoy most? Why?

5. If you could say anything to Frog or Toad, what would you like to say?

Reading/Language Arts

1. Work with students to create a new adventure for Frog and Toad. Students may wish to dictate or write an original story to share with other students.

2. Encourage students to write a letter to Toad. What would they want to say? Make a mailbox from a milk carton or small box that has been painted red and blue. Write a letter back to students taking on the role of Toad.

3. Students may enjoy reading other books about Frog and Toad, including *Frog and Toad All Year*, *Days with Frog and Toad*, and *The Frog and Toad Pop-Up Book*.

Science/Health

1. Students can learn a lot about the growth and development of frogs when they raise a group of tadpoles at school or home. Depending on the species, they will be able to observe the changes a tadpole undergoes (metamorphosis) over a period of several weeks. The directions below will help them create a simple viewing aquarium.

From *The Integrated Curriculum, Second Edition.* © 1998 Anthony D. Fredericks. Teacher Ideas Press. (800) 237-6124.

Materials

> frog's eggs
> a long-handled net (available at any pet store)
> a large glass jar (an oversized mayonnaise jar works well)
> magnifying lens
> pond plants

Procedure

Visit a pond in spring and obtain clumps of jelly-covered frog eggs (about 1–2 dozen eggs), pond water, and pond plants. Put the eggs in a large plastic sandwich bag along with some pond water.

Upon returning to the classroom, fill a clean jar about three-quarters full with pond water. Put the eggs in the jar and place the jar in a location away from direct sunlight. Make sure the water is always room temperature; even a few minutes in direct sunlight can be harmful for developing frogs.

Invite students to use the hand lens and observe the eggs twice a day for a week. Encourage them to record what the eggs look like and how they are developing. Invite them to record their observations in a journal.

The eggs will hatch in about a week. It is important to be very watchful from now on. Don't keep large and small tadpoles in the same jar. The large ones will eat the small ones and hatched tadpoles will snack on unhatched eggs. Students can keep about six tadpoles in a one-gallon jar.

If students are planning to keep their pets until they develop into full-grown adults, they should plan to get a ten-gallon aquarium tank and turn it into a micro-ecosystem.

If you are not able to obtain frog eggs in your local area, you can order the *Grow a Frog* kit (catalog no. 54-110-0296) from Delta Education, P.O. Box 3000, Nashua, NH 03061-3000 [1-800-282-9560]. This kit costs about $15.00 (at this writing) and includes a frog house, food, instructions, and a coupon for tadpoles.

Art

1. Draw and cut out an oversized outline of a toad's body from stiff cardboard or oaktag. Invite students to illustrate the toad in accordance with the illustrations in the book or with those in informational books obtained in the library. Encourage students to record information on toads specifically and amphibians generally that can be written inside the toad's outline.

2. Cut off the fingers from a pair of inexpensive work gloves. Invite students to use a variety of art materials (crayons, yarn, felt-tip pens, sequins, etc.) to turn each "finger" into a puppet representing one of the characters in the book. Students can use these puppets as part of a finger play they create or they can display them in an appropriate "museum" in the classroom.

Math

1. Invite students to create a "world's record" book of frog and toad measurements. Encourage them to conduct some library research in response to the following and to record their results on an oversized classroom chart:

---

    a.   World's largest frog:

    b.   World's largest toad:

    c.   World's smallest frog:

    d.   World's smallest toad:

    e.   Longest leap by a frog:

    f.   Longest period of hibernation by a frog:

    g.   Most number of eggs laid by a toad or frog:

    h.   Longest underwater time by a frog:

    i.   Fastest frog:

    j.   Slowest frog:

2.   Invite students to do some "frog jumping." Working with partners, students can mark a starting line. They can begin by measuring their partner's height and, based on that height, predict how far that person will be able to "long jump." After predicting, they can make several jumps and record the results in a notebook. You may wish to ask the following questions: 1) How close were the predictions to the actual length of the leaps? 2) Was there any relationship between a person's height and how far he or she was able to leap? 3) Did any student leap 40 times his or her height? The results can be posted on a large poster under the heading "Can you out-jump a FROG?"

Music

1.   Invite students as a class to generate a list of frog and toad characteristics (jump, hop, croak, etc.) and use this list to create a class amphibian song set to the tune of a popular children's song. For example (to the tune of "Old MacDonald"):

> Old Mac Donald had a swamp
> E-I-E-I-O
> And in this swamp he had a frog
> E-I-E-I-O
> With a jump, jump here
> And a hop, hop there
> Here a jump
> There a hop
> Everywhere a jump, hop
> Old MacDonald had a swamp
> E-I-E-I-O

Social Studies

1.   Students may wish to create a "frog and toad museum." Collect several artifacts as mentioned in the stories (e.g., buttons, a letter, a bathing suit). Place these in a large flat box (one can be obtained from a nearby bakery). Label each artifact according to which story it is in. Cover the box with clear kitchen wrap so that it looks like a museum case.

From *The Integrated Curriculum, Second Edition.* © 1998 Anthony D. Fredericks. Teacher Ideas Press. (800) 237-6124.

2. Invite students to make a list of all the different types of animals used to advertise commercial products (tigers, bears, cats, etc.). How many different animals are there? Do any commercial products (cereals, cars, toys) use frogs or toads as symbols?

Physical Education

1. Set up a "frog and toad olympics" in which the activities mimic those of frogs and toads, for example, leaping (jumping for distance), sitting on a lily pad (balancing on a suspended mat), and catching flies (catching balls). Invite students to create additional events.

2. Divide the class into two teams and initiate a series of leapfrog races around the room or on the playground.

I Know an Old Lady
Rose Bonne
New York: Rand McNally, 1961

Summary

This is the story of one very unusual lady who has the nasty habit of swallowing animals. In the end, a horse finally does the old lady in. A delightful story that children have enjoyed for ages.

Critical Thinking Questions

1. Why do you think the old lady ate all the animals?

2. What would you do if you swallowed a fly?

3. What other animals might she have swallowed?

4. What animal do you think she could have swallowed to catch the horse?

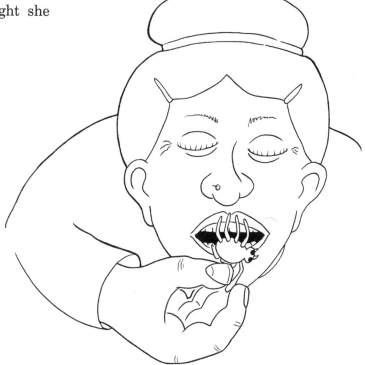

Reading/Language Arts

1. Invite students to tell you a story as if one of the animals from the story were telling it. For example: "My name is Sammy Spider and I did not appreciate being swallowed by the old lady. I wriggled and wriggled and tickled inside her because I was trying to escape." You may want to tape-record some of these stories for playback at a later time.

2. Here are two collections of poetry your students will surely enjoy: *Insectasides* (illustrated by Martha Paulos) (New York: Viking, 1995) and *What to Do When a Bug Climbs in Your Mouth* by Rick Walton (New York: Lothrop, Lee & Shepard, 1995).

3. Invite each student to choose an animal to study. Students can pretend they are writing a newspaper announcement for the birth of their animal. They will need to do some research to collect necessary information. Provide the birth announcement section from daily newspapers for students to use as a reference. Decorate a bulletin board to look like a section of a newspaper and hang the animal birth announcements there. Students can include an illustration of the new "baby."

4. Encourage students to keep an animal journal, a record of all the animals they see during the week. It should include pets, wild animals, insects, and animals seen on television. Hang posters for mammals, fish, birds, reptiles and amphibians, and so on. Students can add to the charts daily.

5. Focus on a different group of animals each day: Monday, insects; Tuesday, fish; Wednesday, carnivores; and so forth. Each day include stories, songs, student-created plays, trivia, games, and environmental concerns related to the animal group. Invite a speaker from the community or local college to discuss current issues relating to the animals.

Science/Health

1. Invite students to brainstorm on different types of animals. Show the National Geographic filmstrip *Fins, Feathers, Fur: Animal Groups* (Educational Services Catalog, filmstrip no. 30619). This film shows how to classify animals by groups. Using the information from the filmstrip, students can create a semantic web categorizing the animals they have researched.

2. Invite students to create a variety of bird feeders and hang them in various locations around the schoolyard. They can keep a record of numbers and varieties of birds in the area over an extended period of time. Following are several possible bird feeders:

   a. Tie a string to a pinecone. Fill the crevices in the cone with peanut butter and roll the cone in some bird seed. Hang the cone from a tree branch.

   b. Cut a large section from the side of a waxed or plastic milk carton. Fill with bird seed and hang from a branch.

   c. Tie several pieces of orange peel onto lengths of string. Hang these in various locations in a nearby tree.

   d. Tie some unsalted peanuts onto various lengths of string. Hang these in a tree.

3. Invite students to create their own classroom terrariums. Provide each of several groups with a clean, two-liter plastic soda bottle (cut off the top beforehand). Ask students to cover the bottom with a layer of small pebbles mixed with bits of charcoal (aquarium charcoal from a pet supply center works well). Then add a layer of soil (about twice as deep as the first layer) in the bottle. Sprinkle the soil with just enough water to keep it moist. Place several plants such as mosses, ferns, lichens, and liverworts in the soil. Grass seed may be sprinkled, too. Place several rocks or pieces of wood in the bottle. Add small land animals (e.g., snails, earthworms). Cover the top (to allow humidity to build up), ventilate, and keep out of direct sunlight. Invite students to record observations over a period of time.

Art

1. Invite students to select their favorite animal from the story. Encourage them to draw a picture of that animal in the process of being eaten by the old lady and another of the animal eating her. Be sure to post the two pictures side by side. Talk about any similarities or differences in the two illustrations. Invite students to tell how the story would change if their animals ate the old lady.

2. Provide students with some modeling clay (available in any hobby store). Work with them to make small models of each of the animals mentioned in the story. These can be displayed in a special place in the classroom.

3. Invite students to look through several old magazines, cut out pictures of the animals mentioned in the story, and put together a scrapbook of "old lady" animals. Students may also want to add pictures of animals that could have been eaten by the old lady.

4. Invite youngsters to locate animal tracks in soft dirt or mud (these can be cat or dog tracks or those of a deer or some other wild animal in your area). Place a circle of cardboard around the track and push it partway down into the soil (be careful not to disturb the track). Mix some plaster of paris according to the package directions. Pour it into the mold up to the top of the cardboard strip. Wait until the plaster cast hardens and remove the cast from the ground print. Take off the cardboard strip and clean off the bottom. Students may wish to make several of these (each of a separate animal) and display them in the classroom along with pertinent research notes.

Math

1. Invite students to create a chart that lists measurements of the following:
   a. The largest fly:
   b. The smallest fly:
   c. The largest spider:
   d. The smallest spider:
   e. The largest bird:
   f. The smallest bird:
   g. Largest and smallest fish, dog, cat, etc.

2. Invite students to weigh and measure their pets at home. They can bring that information to class and record it in a large book. Encourage students to continually update the information throughout the school year.

Music

1. Invite small groups of students to create an "advertising song or ditty" for their favorite animal or group of animals. Class members can describe the features or characteristics that would be most appropriate for the promotion of their selected animal(s).

Social Studies

1. Invite youngsters to keep a journal of the activities, habits, travels, and motions of a single animal. Kids may want to select a house pet or some other animal that can be observed quite regularly throughout the day. Provide youngsters with a field journal—a simple notebook wildlife biologists frequently use to track the activities of one or more wild animals over the course of an extended period of time. Invite students to discuss the daily activities of an animal in comparison with their own daily activities.

2. Invite youngsters to each take on the role of an animal. Encourage them to do the necessary library research on the habits and behaviors of their selected animals. Then have each student write a diary entry—as his or her selected animal might record it—on a day in the life of that species. How does that diary compare with one they might write for themselves?

Physical Education

1. Have a question-and-answer relay. After students create a series of questions pertaining to animals mentioned in the book, they place them in two large containers. Divide the class into two teams. One team member runs to the opposite side of the playground, randomly chooses a question, reads and answers it out loud, and runs back to the team. A second person repeats the process until all team members have completed the course. The first team to finish and answer all the questions correctly is the winner.

Jack and the Beanstalk
Lorinda Bryan Cauley
New York: G. P. Putnam's Sons, 1983

Summary

This is the classic story of Jack, a handful of magic beans, and a mean giant. In the end, good wins out over evil and Jack and his mother live happily ever after.

Critical Thinking Questions

1. Do you think Jack was right or wrong in taking the hen and the golden harp from the giant?

2. What would you do if you came across a hen that lays golden eggs?

3. How do you think your family would react if you came home with some magic beans?

Reading/Language Arts

1. Before reading this book to students invite them to look at the cover of the book and guess what it is about. Ask students if they have ever heard some or all of this story. What do they know about giants and magical things?

2. Invite students to invent a new version of the story as told from the giant's point of view. How does he feel about Jack taking his hen and golden harp? Is there another way of telling the story so that *everyone* lives happily ever after?

3. Invite an employee of a local garden center or nursery to visit the classroom and discuss the types of plants that are native to your area. What are some planting techniques? How should plants be cared for? Why are some plants easier to grow than others? Invite students to gather the responses to those questions as well as their own into an informative brochure or leaflet that could be distributed at the garden center or nursery.

Science/Health

1. Invite students to grow their own beanstalks. Obtain some pole bean seeds from a local nursery or garden center. Plant two or three in each of several paper cups filled with potting soil. Water each cup and place them on a window ledge or in sunlight. Place a straight stick or ruler in each cup. Ask students to note any growth. As the seeds sprout and begin to grow, measure their height over a period of several days and weeks. Talk about the speed at which the beans are growing and the elements they need to survive. Students may wish to take some photographs of the beans at different stages of their growth. These can be placed into a special scrapbook.

2. Obtain two similar potted plants (of equal vigor and height). Invite students to select 20 random leaves on one plant. Ask students to smear a thin layer of petroleum jelly on the tops of ten leaves and the bottoms of ten other leaves (on the same plant). Place both plants on a windowsill and water and fertilize as necessary. After several days invite students to observe the two plants and note any differences. What happened to the leaves with petroleum jelly on the top? What happened to the leaves with petroleum jelly on the bottom? What can this tell us about some of the processes of plants?

3. Obtain two similar potted plants (of equal vigor and height). Water and fertilize the plants as necessary. Invite one student to place a large, clear cellophane bag over the top of one plant, securing it around the pot with a rubber band (the bag should be as airtight as possible around the plant). Place the plants on a windowsill. After several days, encourage students to note what happens inside the bagged plant. Students may wish to occasionally remove the bag from that plant and measure the amount of water that is transpired by the plant every two days (for example). Be sure to keep both plants adequately watered.

Art

1. Invite students to invent and design an appropriate comic strip for this book. The strip can be a summarization of the major events in the story or a pictorial representation of students' favorite sections.

2. Invite students to create a three-dimensional collage of important artifacts mentioned in the story. Encourage students to collect artifacts from home to be affixed to a large piece of cardboard and developed into an oversized display. Next to each artifact, students can designate the book page on which it is first mentioned.

Math

1. If possible, invite students to grow several bean plants in the classroom (see the Science/Health section). Encourage them to keep a chart or graph of each plant's growth over an extended period of time (one month, two months). Invite students to develop line graphs of each plant's growth and share them with class members.

2. Following is a recipe for bean soup that will serve 12 people. Invite students to calculate the quantities of each ingredient in order for the recipe to serve everyone in the class, everyone in your grade, or everyone in the school.

✂ *Bean Soup*

INGREDIENTS

1 lb. of navy or kidney beans	1 tbsp. flour
4 qts. water	2 tbsp. water
½ lb. salt pork	salt and pepper to taste
1 large onion, cut coarsely	2 tbsp. chopped parsley
4 stalks celery, cut coarsely	

DIRECTIONS

Soak the beans in 2 quarts of water overnight. The next day, add the remaining water, pork, onion, and celery. Bring to a boil, cover, and simmer for 1½ hours. Remove the pork and cut into small pieces. Press the bean mixture through a sieve, return to heat, and add the pork. Combine flour and 2 tablespoons of water and stir into the soup. Season with salt, pepper, and parsley. Ladle into bowls.

✂ -

Music

1. Invite students to record music from various television shows that could be used as background music for a retelling of this story. For example, suspenseful music (from a detective show) could be played as Jack is climbing the beanstalk. "Chase music" (from a crime drama) could be played as the giant is chasing Jack.

Social Studies

1. Folktales often reflect a culture's traditions, customs, and values. Read aloud folktales from various cultures. After each tale is read, discuss what students have learned about the culture and invite them to complete a profile similar to the following. What similarities and what differences can be found?

	Book 1	Book 2	Book 3
Title:			
Country of origin:			
Details about life:			
Values & attitudes:			
Customs:			
Other:			

---

2. Many folktales lend themselves to being acted out in a mock trial. For example, Hansel and Gretel can be charged with trespassing or the wolf in "Little Red Riding Hood" can be charged with impersonating Grandma. Invite students to develop a mock trial for either Jack (trespassing) or the giant (destruction of property) and to share it with another class.

Physical Education

1. Invite the PE teacher or a coach from the local high school to demonstrate rope-climbing skills. What are some exercises that can be used to help develop muscles used in rope-climbing? Invite students to test their rope-climbing abilities in the gym. What difficulties do they note? What kinds of difficulties would Jack have in climbing the beanstalk?

Leo the Late Bloomer
Robert Kraus
New York: Windmill Books, 1971

Summary

Leo the tiger takes his time growing up. His parents are patient and eventually he does begin to bloom.

Critical Thinking Questions

1. What makes Leo such an interesting character?

2. How would you feel if you were a late bloomer?

3. What does the term *late bloomer* mean to you?

4. If you were Leo's friend, how would you treat him?

5. What part of the book would you change if you could? Why?

Reading/Language Arts

1. Obtain a large sheet of newsprint (available at most art or hobby stores). Invite students to lie down on the paper while classmates trace their outlines. Have the children cut out their outlines and write (or dictate for you to write) words that best describe each student. Place these words randomly within the outline and hang each one in the classroom. Encourage students to think of other words to be added to the outline periodically and note that the descriptive words vary from individual to individual—indicating that each student is unique.

Science/Health

1. Invite students to plant a bean or radish seed in a paper cup filled with potting soil. Point out that though students can't see the seed growing inside the soil, eventually it will germinate and grow. Students can observe the cup every other day and keep a journal on the growth of the seed. Invite students to compare the hidden growth of the seed to Leo's hidden growth.

2. Here's an experiment that will help students learn about what seeds need to begin growing.

Materials

36 radish seeds	water
six plastic sandwich bags	candle wax
paper towels (cut in half)	marker

Procedure

Invite students to place pieces of paper towel in the bottom of sandwich bags as directed below. Place six radish seeds between layers of the paper towel in each bag (leave the bags open). Label each bag with a number and then finish setting up each bag as follows:

Bag 1: moistened paper towel, no light (put in a drawer or closet), room temperature.

Bag 2: paper towel, water, light, room temperature.

Bag 3: dry paper towel, light, room temperature.

Bag 4: no paper towel (seeds floating in water), light, room temperature.

Bag 5: paper towel, water, no light, keep in refrigerator or freezer.

Bag 6: dry paper towel, no light, room temperature, seeds covered by candle wax.

Invite students to record the date and time they began this activity and check each of the bags twice daily for any changes.

Eventually, students will note that the seeds in Bag 1 and Bag 2 begin to germinate. There may be some minor change in the seeds in Bag 4. Discuss with them that seeds need favorable temperature, adequate moisture, and oxygen to germinate. Light is not needed.

Encourage students to compare the conditions necessary for a plant to begin growing (sprouting) and those necessary for a child to begin growing. What are the similarities and differences?

Art

1. Students may enjoy making casts of their feet or hands. This can be done with the following recipe for flour dough:

✂ *Flour Dough*

INGREDIENTS

2 c. self-rising flour

2 tbsp. alum

2 tbsp. salt

2 tbsp. cooking oil

1 c. + 2 tbsp. boiling water

DIRECTIONS

Carefully mix all ingredients and then knead until consistency is doughy. Roll out some of the mixture for each child to press a hand or foot into. Put the cast outside in the sun or bake in a slow oven (250 degrees) for several hours. Students can paint their casts, keep them for several months, and then make additional ones if they wish to measure their growth during that time period.

Math

1. Invite students to create personal timelines of important learning events in their lives. When did they learn to walk, talk, read, or draw? Long strips of adding-machine paper can be affixed to a bulletin board with each student recording his or her significant life events. The emphasis is not on comparing students but rather on that certain events occur at different times in people's lives.

2. Invite students to weigh and measure themselves. The data can be plotted on a large classroom chart. A separate chart can also be prepared on the various heights and weights of family pets.

Music

1. Invite students to think of a theme song for this book. What popular tune would be most appropriate as background music when reading the book aloud to others? Encourage students to defend their choices.

Social Studies

1. Invite students to talk with various family members about when they learned to walk, talk, write, read, and draw. What differences do youngsters note? Are there any patterns or does it seem as though everyone grows and learns at completely different rates?

Physical Education

1. Invite the school nurse or a local doctor to visit your classroom to discuss some of the developmental stages of youngsters. What are some physical activities that students at your grade level should be able to do? Make sure the emphasis is on the fact that not everyone develops at the same rate but rather that there are averages to help gauge proper development.

2. Students may wish to have short, timed running races. These can be repeated at selected intervals throughout the school year. Plan time to discuss with students that their times may show improvement simply because they are developing important skills. The emphasis should not be on the competitive aspects of the races but rather on the fact that each youngster will improve, grow, and develop at a rate different from everyone else throughout the year.

The Three Bears
Paul Galdone
New York: Seabury, 1972

Summary

This is the traditional story of Goldilocks and the three bears. It details the adventures (or misadventures) of Goldilocks as she breaks into the bears' house. Delightful illustrations highlight this retelling.

Critical Thinking Questions

1. If you were the little wee bear, how would you have felt about Goldilocks eating all your porridge, breaking your chair, and messing up your bed?

2. What do you think the bears would have done to Goldilocks if she had not run away?

3. Do you think the three bears will leave their door unlocked next time? Why?

4. What would you do if you found somebody strange sleeping in your bed?

5. Would you like to have Goldilocks as a friend? Why or why not?

Reading/Language Arts

1. Invite students to create a sequel to this story, such as one titled "Goldilocks Returns." What types of adventures would Goldilocks have on the return visit?

2. Encourage students to pretend that there are three Goldilocks and one bear. How would the story change? Invite students to dictate or write a new version of the tale.

3. Invite the class to produce and put on a play about Goldilocks and the three bears. Only simple props (chairs, beds, bowls, etc.) are necessary. If possible, videotape the play and show it to other classes.

4. Invite students to identify the number of times the word *bear* shows up in the names of commercial products (bear cereal, bear cookies). Encourage students to make a list of various product names with *bear*.

5. Here are four excellent books about bears that you may wish to share with students: *Bears for Kids* by Jeff Fair (Minocqua, WI: NorthWord Press, 1991); *Great Crystal Bear* by Carolyn Lesser (San Diego, CA: Harcourt Brace, 1996); *Bears* by Malcom Penny (New York: Bookwright Press, 1990); and *Bears* by Kate Petty (New York: Gloucester Press, 1991).

Science/Health

1. The National Geographic Society (P.O. Box 96580, Washington, DC 20077-9964 [1-800-343-6610]) produces several wonderful videos including *Polar Bear Alert* (catalog no. 51290), *Giant Bears of Kodiak Island* (catalog no. 51654), *The Grizzlies* (catalog no. 51300), and *Secrets of the Wild Panda* (catalog no. 51997). If possible, obtain one or more videos and show them to students. Talk with students about the habits, habitats, life cycles, and diets of various species of bears in the wild.

2. Invite students to write letters to the Office of Endangered Species, U.S. Fish and Wildlife Service, Department of the Interior, Washington, DC 20240, to obtain information on the current status of endangered species of bears. When the information arrives, invite students to create special posters to inform the public about the status of specific species.

Art

1. Work with students to make a simple identification card (similar to your driver's license) that could be used in case he or she ever got lost. You may wish to take students to a local police station and talk with one of the officers about what to do whenever someone gets lost. Students may also wish to create a similar form of identification for Goldilocks.

Math

1. Invite students to create a series of bar graphs illustrating the life span of different species of bears. Which species has the longest life span? Which the shortest? Does a bear's life span change when it is confined at a zoo or wildlife animal park? Students may wish to contact a zoologist or biologist at a nearby college to obtain answers.

Music

1. Invite students to work with the music teacher to put together a collection of songs that refer to bears (e.g., "The Bear Came over the Mountain").

Social Studies

1. Invite students to form small groups and research various bear legends and tales in different countries or cultures. Students may wish to duplicate stories and gather them into a bound book (e.g., "Bear Legends of Native Americans"). Some students may wish to examine various bear constellations (e.g., *Ursa major*) and report their findings to the class.

Physical Education

1. Because bears seem to spend a lot of time resting or hibernating, an exercise program might be beneficial for them. Invite students to assemble an exercise book for bears. They can check with the PE teacher for some suitable exercises or activities that would help bears maintain their conditioning through the winter (but still allow them to maintain their fat stores so they do not go hungry).

2. Invite students to participate in "bear walk" races. A "bear walk" requires students to walk with their hands and feet on the floor at the same time.

The Very Hungry Caterpillar
Eric Carle
New York: Crowell, 1976

Summary

The caterpillar is born on a leaf. It goes through the week eating different foods until it is so full, it builds a cocoon. Finally it hatches into a beautiful butterfly. This book introduces the life cycle of the butterfly, the days of the week, and nutrition in a simple way.

Critical Thinking Questions

1. What part of the story did you enjoy most?

2. What else would you like to learn about caterpillars?

3. What are some of your favorite foods?

4. If you could change into something else, what would it be?

Reading/Language Arts

1. Drape a sheet over a clothesline or between two chairs. Crawl inside with one or more students and retell the story. Discuss how it might feel to be inside a cocoon for an extended period of time.

2. Encourage students to write a sequel to *The Very Hungry Caterpillar* about its life as a butterfly.

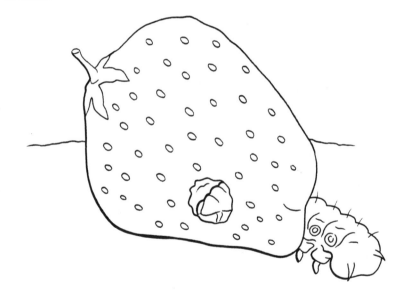

3. Cut large sheets of paper into simple butterfly shapes. Invite students to write a brief paragraph that begins, "If I were a butterfly, I . . ." Encourage students to share their stories and then compile them into a class booklet.

Science/Health

1. Take students for a walk around the school to look for caterpillars. They can usually be found on trees in warm weather. Students can collect them in jars to observe later. Invite students to observe and record how they act in their natural environment. Students may also wish to decorate their jars with fabric, paint pens, and ribbon.

2. Students may enjoy observing how different kinds of animals grow and mature. The following specialized containers (and the accompanying animals and creatures) can be obtained through the mail from Delta Education (P.O. Box 950, Hudson, NH 03051 [1-800-442-5444]).

    a. Aquaria/terraria (catalog no. 57-200-6256). Includes coupons for goldfish, tadpoles, hermit crab, or chameleon—$24.95.

    b. The Bug House (catalog no. 57-020-8086)—$5.65.

    c. Critter City (catalog no. 57-031-6557)—$24.95.

    d. Fruit Flies, Mealworms, & Butterflies Mini-Kit (catalog no. 57-740-0096). Includes coupon for living organisms—$89.95.

    e. Butterfly Garden (catalog no. 57-716-0010). Includes coupon for 25 larvae—$44.95.

    f. Giant Ant Farm (catalog no. 57-010-2310). Includes coupon for ants—$19.95.

    g. Grow a Frog (catalog no. 57-110-0296). Includes a coupon for tadpoles—$14.95.

3. Some people collect butterflies. Try to locate someone with a butterfly collection who will share it with your class. If this is not possible, obtain a copy of *Butterflies Are Beautiful* by Ruth Brin (Minneapolis, MN: Lerner, 1974) or similar books that contain excellent illustrations of butterflies. Encourage students to look at the different kinds of butterflies. Plan time to discuss their differences and similarities.

4. Students may enjoy hearing about some of the different types of caterpillars from around the world. An excellent resource is *Creepy, Crawly Caterpillars* by Margery Facklam (Boston: Little, Brown, 1996).

Art

1. Provide students with jelly beans, tiny eyes (small pieces of licorice), small pieces of pipe cleaners, and a toothpick. Students can make their own caterpillars by sticking the jelly beans on the toothpick. Students can then put the pipe cleaners in the head and glue the eyes on.

2. Invite children to bring their baby pictures to class. Make photocopies of the pictures and have students glue the copies on large sheets of paper. Have the students use their picture as the head of a caterpillar, drawing the caterpillar's body on the paper. Students can illustrate the body with colored crayons or watercolor paints. Be sure to display the pictures.

3. Provide students with egg cartons cut in half lengthwise. Invite students to paint them. When the cartons are dry, have students make a face on one end and insert pipe cleaners for feelers. The result—a classroom full of caterpillars.

Math

1. Invite students to collect caterpillars from around the school and place each one in the middle of a sheet of graph paper. Invite students to record the length of time it takes the caterpillar to travel five squares, 10 squares, or to the end of the sheet. Which caterpillars are faster? Invite students to chart and record their findings.

From *The Integrated Curriculum, Second Edition*. © 1998 Anthony D. Fredericks. Teacher Ideas Press. (800) 237-6124.

Music

1. Various musical instruments sound "slow." For example, bassoons and cellos are usually played in a slow, methodical manner. Invite the music teacher to visit your classroom (or obtain a series of introductory music recordings) to demonstrate several different musical instruments. Ask students to select those that would be most appropriate in "describing" the movements of a caterpillar. Then invite them to select instruments whose sound would best describe the movements of a butterfly.

Social Studies

1. Invite students to put together an identification guide for various caterpillars from around the world. What types of caterpillars can be found in Africa, in Europe, in South America, in Asia, or in North America? Students may wish to draw illustrations of various species of caterpillars and post them on a large map of the world.

2. Several species of caterpillars live and work together in very large groups (e.g., tent caterpillars, bagworms, processionary caterpillars). Discuss with students the advantages of caterpillars working together in a group. What similarities are there in group work among caterpillars and among in human beings?

Physical Education

1. Invite students to conduct "caterpillar races." In these races, students must lie on the floor and wriggle to move their bodies across the room (use of hands or feet is not allowed).

The Yucky Reptile Alphabet Book
Jerry Pallotta
Watertown, MA: Charlesbridge, 1989

Summary

This book (one of a series) introduces the letters of the alphabet by describing a reptile for each letter, from the armadillo lizard to the dinosaurs of a zillion years ago.

Critical Thinking Questions

1. Which of the animals in this book is the most interesting?

2. Which of the animals would you like to learn more about?

3. Are there other reptiles you know about that could be included in this book?

4. Which of the reptiles included in this book would you find in your town or state?

Reading/Language Arts

1. Students may enjoy reading other books about reptiles. Here are some particularly good ones: *Alligators* by Frank Staub (Minneapolis, MN: Lerner, 1996); *Reptiles* by Allen Greer (New York: Time-Life, 1996); *Snakes, Salamanders and Lizards* by Diane Burns (Minocqua, WI: NorthWord Press, 1995); and *Weird Walkers* by Anthony D. Fredericks (Minocqua, WI: NorthWord Press, 1996).

2. Invite each student in the class to select one of the reptiles illustrated in the book. Encourage each child to conduct necessary library research on his or her identified species. Then, invite each student to write a series of diary entries told from the perspective of the creature, for example, "A Day in the Life of a Leatherback Turtle" or "My Life as a Gila Monster."

Science/Health

1. Contact a zoologist or herpetologist at the biology or zoology department of a local college or university. Make arrangements for a visit to the campus so that students have an opportunity to talk with and ask questions of a "reptile expert." Have students prepare their questions ahead of time. After the trip, invite students to select one or more of the following projects based on what they learned:

   a. Invite a group of students to create a newsletter or newspaper describing the trip.

   b. Encourage students to design a brochure on important points learned during the visit. The brochure can be distributed to other youngsters or attached as part of the book.

   c. Invite students to create a "care and feeding" manual on selected reptiles seen during the visit. How should these creatures be cared for while in captivity?

   d. Some students may wish to put together a news broadcast about the trip and what was learned during the visit.

Art

1. Students may enjoy preparing the following snack:

✂ *Yummy Reptiles*

INGREDIENTS

2 c. peanut butter
4 tbsp. honey
1 c. nonfat dry milk

8 tbsp. toasted wheat germ
unsweetened cocoa powder
sliced almonds

DIRECTIONS

In a bowl, mix peanut butter and honey. Stir in dry milk and wheat germ until well blended. Lay waxed paper on a baking sheet. Using 1–3 tablespoons at a time, form peanut butter mixture into the shapes of selected reptiles from the book. Put on baking sheet. Dip a toothpick in cocoa powder and press lightly across the top of the "reptiles" to make various body patterns. Stick on almonds for tongues, scales, or legs. Chill for 30 minutes.

✂ -

Math

1. Invite students to put together a chart or graph of the world's fastest reptiles. After necessary library research, students can assemble data relating to the speeds of selected species. This information can be presented on an oversized sheet of cardboard or oaktag. Additional data, such as the following, can also be added:

   a. World's fastest reptile:

   b. World's biggest reptile:

   c. World's longest reptile:

   d. World's heaviest reptile:

Music

1. Invite students to listen to "Flight of the Bumblebee" by Rimsky-Korsakov. Ask them to imagine the scenes taking place as they listen. What instruments create the illusion of bumblebees? What other animal sounds can be created with musical instruments? Does any instrument imitate the sound of a reptile in this book?

Social Studies

1. Invite students to post an oversized map of the world on a bulletin board or large wall. Encourage them to write the names of each of the 26 reptiles on separate index cards and post these cards around the edges of the map. Using lengths of yarn, they can attach one end to a card and the other end to the country or continent in which the animal lives. Students may wish to work in groups to conduct necessary library research on selected animals and their respective environments prior to posting the cards.

Physical Education

1. Invite students to simulate the movement of various reptiles identified in this book. How would a gecko, moloch, or Komodo dragon move across the floor? Invite students to discuss some of the difficulties they have in simulating the movements of those creatures. What adaptations do they need to make to accurately portray selected animals?

GRADE 3

Alexander and the Terrible, Horrible, No Good, Very Bad Day

Judith Viorst
New York: Macmillan, 1972

Summary

One day Alexander wakes up with gum in his hair. From then on the whole day is filled with one misfortune after another. He wants to move to Australia, but he realizes terrible days happen everywhere, even in Australia.

Critical Thinking Questions

1. If you were Alexander, what would you have done to change the day?

2. Could any of the other characters have helped Alexander so that he would have a good day?

3. Does everybody have bad days? Why?

4. Is Alexander's day similar to any day you have had? How did you deal with your "very bad day"?

Reading/Language Arts

1. Invite each student to write a brief essay (in the classroom) about a recent horrible day. What happened? How did they feel? Ask each student to share the essay with other class members. Did the others see the "terrible day" in the same way the writer did?

2. Encourage students to create an alternate version of the story entitled "Alexander and the Wonderful, Terrific, Super, Fantastic Day." Students may wish to record the story on tape or write it for other students to enjoy.

3. Have students pretend to be advice columnists. Encourage them to suggest some strategies or solutions for Alexander to consider in dealing with his terrible day.

4. Invite students to interview an adult about the worst day that individual ever had. Students may want to interview a parent, babysitter, or neighbor. Encourage students to take notes during the interview. Invite individual students to share their interviews with the rest of the class.

5. This book focuses on some of the various machines and mechanical devices in Alexander's life. Students may be interested in reading books about machines and how they are used. The following are excellent: *Machines at Work* by Byron Barton (New York: Crowell, 1987); *Invention* by Lionel Bender (New York: Knopf,

---

1991); *Force: The Power Behind Movement* by Eric Laithwaite (New York: Watts, 1986); *The Way Things Work* by David Macauley (Boston: Houghton Mifflin, 1988); *Everyday Things and How They Work* by Steve Parker (New York: Random House, 1991); *Machines and Movement* by Barbara Taylor (New York: Warwick Press, 1990); and *Machines and How They Work* by Harvey Weiss (New York: Crowell, 1983).

Science/Health

1. Invite students to make a technology timeline. Provide them with a long sheet of newsprint taped to one wall of the classroom. Encourage students to record the dates of major technological advances (and provide accompanying illustrations), particularly those involving the development of machines. Invite students to consult the references in the school or public library. Following are a few examples to get them started:

    a. Discovery of the wheel, 3500 B.C.
    b. Sails and sailboats, 5000–3200 B.C.
    c. Sundial, 500 B.C.
    d. Mechanical clock, A.D. 725
    e. Development of horse-drawn vehicles, A.D. 800–900
    f. Printing press, 1454
    g. Spinning wheel, 1530
    h. Steam engine, 1700s
    i. Cotton gin, 1793
    j. Bicycle, 1816
    k. Internal combustion engine, 1880

2. Students may wish to create their own "car" with the following activity:

    Push one end of a rubber band through the hole in a spool of thread (using a large paper clip that has been straightened out). When one end of the rubber band pokes out of the other end of the spool, slip it onto a medium-sized paper clip. Tape this clip to the far end of the spool.

    Slip the rubber band at the near end of the spool through a jumbo paper clip. Turn this clip to twist the rubber band, being careful that it doesn't bunch inside the spool. After the rubber band is twisted, keep winding for about 15–25 additional turns.

    Place the "car" on a table top or other flat surface, release it and stand back. It will dash across the surface. A rubber band wrapped around the middle of the spool will provide more traction for the "car."

Art

1. In the book, Alexander created a picture of an invisible castle. Challenge students to come up with their own versions of an invisible castle. What would it look like? What colors (if any) could be used? How would an illustration of an invisible castle differ from a picture of a real castle? Is the castle invisible or is the illustration invisible?

Math

1. Invite students to create an imaginary timeline of all the activities and events in this story. They can print selected events along a length of adding-machine tape. Over each event a selected time of day can be printed as well. Encourage students to defend their choice of times and the corresponding event(s). The strips of paper can be posted on a bulletin board.

Music

1. Invite students to create a song especially for Alexander. What type of tune or lyrics would be most appropriate for someone who is really having a terrible, horrible, no good, very bad day? Are there any popular songs that would summarize Alexander's day and the things that happened to him?

Social Studies

1. Invite students to obtain some materials and resources on Australia from the library. Encourage them to put together a descriptive brochure (sheets of paper stapled together) on the climate, animals, lifestyles, geography, and other aspects of the country. What are some factors about Australia that make it unique?

2. Invite students to make a list of inventions discussed in the book. Encourage them to describe how people might be able to live or survive without those inventions.

Physical Education

1. Invite students to create a list of all the physical activities that took place in this book. Afterward, encourage them to create another list that includes all those activities or sports that require the use of sneakers (similar to what Alexander bought). Another list of sports that do not require sneakers can also be prepared. You may want to ask students the following riddle: In what sport do the participants wear iron shoes? (Answer: horse racing.)

The Bathwater Gang

Jerry Spinelli
Boston: Little, Brown, 1990

Summary

Bertie's gang of girls and Andy's gang of boys were always at war. One day, during a particularly intense mud fight, the two gangs discovered, through Granny, that they could join forces to form a single gang with one very productive purpose.

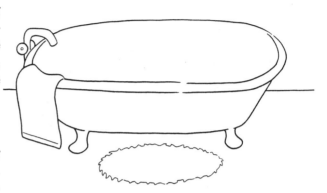

Critical Thinking Questions

1. In the story, Damaris's mother is described as a flower child. What do you think flower children are and how do you think they got that name?

2. Bertie creates a platform that lists the beliefs of her gang. What items would you include in your list of beliefs? Why are these things important to you?

3. Bertie's and Andy's gangs are rather mean to each other while they are at war. What are some tricks that could have been used instead of the ones in the book?

4. Why do you think Granny doesn't feel that gangs are bad but Damaris's mother does?

5. What would have happened between Bertie's gang and Andy's gang if it had never started raining? Would the mud hole have formed? Would Granny have started the Bathwater Gang?

Reading/Language Arts

1. Invite students to re-create one of the scenes in the book and develop it into a skit. The skit can be presented to another class or group of students. Afterward, encourage students to discuss the advantages of working as a team with a common goal.

2. Appoint several students in the class as newspaper reporters. Invite the reporters to interview several students throughout the school on the advantages and disadvantages of membership in a single-sex group, club, or team. What differences do the reporters note in the responses of girls and boys? Can they draw any conclusions? The results of the interviews may be written up in the form of a newsletter and distributed to all class members.

3. While reading the story out loud to students, stop at the part where Damaris begins to rinse off the unknown person. Invite students to write, in 25 words or less, who they think the individual is. Invite them to pinpoint any story clues that lead them to their conclusion.

4. Invite students to read selected portions of the book in dramatic fashion—that is, in an angry voice, an excited voice, a sad voice, a humorous voice. Encourage

students to practice various "voices" for the same part and discuss the implications of voice inflection on the understanding and appreciation of the story.

5. Invite students to write to a pen pal in another classroom (make prior arrangements with a colleague) concerning the events and situations in the book they enjoyed most. Encourage students to invite their pen pals to respond with questions about the book that can be answered in subsequent letters.

Science/Health

1. Invite students to make a list of the characteristics or habits an animal should have to qualify it as a good household pet. Encourage students to start with the qualities of their own pets and branch out to include features of other animals they are particularly fond of.

2. Invite students to collect various kinds of soil samples from the local community (four or more different soils would be ideal). Put an equal amount of soil and water in plastic cups. Encourage students to make predictions as to which soil would be best for a mud fight. Which soil would be best to use with new plants? Which soil would be best for plants that need very little water? Students may wish to experiment by planting several different varieties of houseplants in their soil samples and recording the growth rates of those plants to determine which soil is most favorable.

3. Students are often fascinated to discover that there are different varieties of rain—from highly acidic rain (acid rain) to highly alkaline rain. Plant several bean seeds in plastic cups filled with potting soil. After the plants have emerged, invite students to water them with identical quantities of different types of water. To one cup of water, add the juice from one lemon; to another, a cup of vinegar; to another, a tablespoon of salt; and to another, nothing. Invite students to chart the results and discuss the implications of their observations.

Art

1. Invite students to create an oversized class mural depicting the battle at the mud hole, the washing of the pets, the pizza party, and other selected story events. Put a small group in charge of illustrating each selected event. The finished mural can be displayed along one wall of the classroom or in the hallway.

2. Obtain one or more refrigerator boxes from a local appliance store. Invite students to decorate each one as though it were a gang's clubhouse. These can be placed in the room and used as reading "centers" for free reading time.

3. Provide students with modeling clay and invite them to create several of the animals mentioned in the story. Students may also wish to create replicas of their own pets.

Math

1. Invite students to create their own word problems using lemonade. For example, if Bertie sold six cups of lemonade at 20 cents a cup, how much money did she make? Encourage students to develop other appropriate problems.

---

2. Invite students to determine how many slices of pizza each girl could eat given that 10 large pizzas were ordered for 59 girls (figure on eight slices per pizza). Students may also wish to determine how many pizzas it would take to feed their class.

3. Invite students to determine Bertie's weekly allowance. Her allowance for the 20 weeks went to her parents to pay for the 10 large pizzas. How much money did Bertie lose?

4. Encourage students to develop ratio and percentage problems regarding how many members signed up for Bertie's gang and how many actually showed up at the pizza party and at the meeting.

Music

1. Invite students to put together a collection of songs that pertain to water or bathing. (Some possible "water" songs include "April Showers," "September in the Rain," and "I'm Forever Blowing Bubbles," all of which can be found in *Family Songbook*, arranged and edited by Dan Fox [Pleasantville, NY: Reader's Digest Association, 1969].) What songs do they sing at home or at camp that include water? What songs have they heard on the radio or TV that have a water theme? Students may wish to interview adults about "water songs" to include in their collection. New songs can be invented and added, too.

Social Studies

1. Discuss with students why people like to belong to groups or gangs. Why are people comfortable in belonging to an "organization"? What benefits are there for the individual? Ask students to list all the "gangs" they belong to (the class, the school, their family, Scouts, a sports team, etc.). Which "gangs" seem to attract the most people? Why?

2. Invite students to design a community map of the area Bertie lives in. What services and buildings are in the town? What are the town's distinctive features? What geographic features are present? Students may elect to create two-dimensional drawings or three-dimensional salt maps.

3. Encourage students to discuss the qualifications necessary to become the leader of an organization or group. What are some necessary leadership skills essential to the smooth running and functioning of a group? Did Bertie have those skills? Invite students to put together a guidebook on how organizations should be run and how a leader should behave as the temporary leader of a classroom group or as the president of the United States.

Physical Education

1. Students can play a modification of Capture the Flag. However, in this version the object is to capture a sheet of paper that has the other team's platform written on it (these will have to be prepared in advance). The gang that can capture the most prisoners and get the platform from the other gang wins the game.

Cow

Jules Older

Watertown, MA: Charlesbridge, 1997

Summary

A lighthearted look at one of our favorite animals. The author introduces us to several breeds of cows, how they eat grass, the anatomy of a cow, and some of the amazing facts about cows around the world. A wonderful book for any reader.

Critical Thinking Questions

1. What was the most amazing thing you learned about cows?

2. Why are cows so important?

3. How is a cow's digestive system similar to or different from your digestive system?

4. What are some of the things you would have to think about if you had a cow for a pet?

Reading/Language Arts

1. Involve students in a "fractured folktale" festival to create new versions of folktales, fairy tales, and Mother Goose rhymes from around the world. In a fractured folktale, one or more elements of the story are changed for humorous effect. Readers theatre (prepared scripts that are read aloud) provides students with creative and imaginative interpretations of familiar stories in a comfortable and engaging format. The following script (from *Tadpole Tales and Other Totally Terrific Treats for Readers Theatre* by Anthony D. Fredericks [Englewood, CO: Teacher Ideas Press, 1997]) would be particularly appropriate as a humorous extension of *Cow*.

Hey, Diddle, Diddle, the Cat and the Fiddle, and the Cow Just Can't Get over the Moon

STAGING: The narrator stands at a lectern or podium. Each of the other characters can stand in a loose semicircle or sit on chairs.

```
                                    Cow
                                     X
                     Cat                       Dog
                      X                          X
             Dish                                        Spoon
              X                                            X
          Fiddle
            X
   Narrator
      X
```

NARRATOR: Once upon a time there was this cow. The cow was part of a well-known Mother Goose story. You've probably heard it. It goes something like this: Hey, diddle, diddle, the cat and the fiddle, the cow jumped over the moon, and so on, and so on, and so on. Well, to tell the truth, the cow really didn't jump over the moon. Let's listen and find out why.

COW: Hey, guys, we've got a real problem. Someone is going to write a Mother Goose rhyme about us, and for it to rhyme, they're going to have me jump over the moon. I mean, can you believe that?

FIDDLE: That's unbelievable, Cow. Why would they want you to jump all the way over the moon?

COW: Well, actually they needed a word that would rhyme with *spoon*.

SPOON: Hey, now, don't blame me. I'm just going to run away with the dish.

DISH: Yeah, that's right. But, you see, these writers couldn't figure out any words that would rhyme with *dish* except for *wish* and *fish*. And I know they don't want anyone running away with a fish.

SPOON: That's why they had to put me at the end of that line.

DOG: Yea, they sure couldn't put me at the end of a line. What would I rhyme with? *Hog*? *Frog*? *Jog*?

FIDDLE:	That's right. Dog is just supposed to laugh in this story. It would change everything if he and a frog ran away.
CAT:	Hey, wait a minute. How is a dish able to talk?
DISH:	Don't worry about it. This is just a Mother Goose rhyme. All kinds of things, from plates to pancakes, can talk in these stories. Don't let it bother you.
CAT:	O.K.
COW:	Now, wait a second, guys. We're getting away from my problem, which is, how am I going to be able to soar over the moon? I'm not a space shuttle you know, and I'm not the lightest animal in the world. So, what do I do?
SPOON:	Maybe we could invent some kind of rocket launcher to get you up in space.
COW:	Do we look like rocket scientists? How are we going to invent a rocket launcher?
DOG:	Well, we can talk, so we must be pretty smart.
DISH:	Yeah, but not smart enough to get fat old Bossy here up into space and up and over the moon.
CAT:	So, what are we going to do?
COW:	I guess we are just going to have to let the writer use his imagination to get me over the moon and back safely so that I can rhyme with my friend the spoon.
NARRATOR:	And so it was. The cow was just too fat to get over the moon in real life. But the writer made up a real neat poem that made you think that the cow could actually jump that high. And this is what he wrote: Hey, diddle, diddle, the cat and the fiddle, The cow jumped over the moon; The little dog laughed to see such a sport, And the dish ran away with the spoon.
COW:	Hey, thanks a lot, guys!

SOURCE: Fredericks, Anthony D. *Tadpole Tales and Other Totally Terrific Treats for Readers Theatre.* Englewood, CO: Teacher Ideas Press, 1997. Used by permission.

Science/Health

1. Cows spend a great deal of time eating grass. Kids spend a great deal of time eating junk food. Invite students to write to the Center for Science in the Public Interest (1875 Connecticut Ave. NW, Ste. 300, Washington, DC 20009) and request information about one or more of the following:

   a. A three-dimensional Healthy Eating Pyramid that rates more than 200 foods.
   b. The Junk Food Jail poster.
   c. The Kids Against Junk Food organization.

   After the materials arrive, plan time to talk with students about the need for a healthy, balanced diet. You may wish to discuss why cows are able to survive on one primary food, whereas growing children need a variety of foods for good health.

2. Invite students to look through several old magazines for photographs of young animals. Encourage them to note the proportion of body parts in several young animals in comparison with adults. For example, young horses' legs seem to be too long, but when they grow up, their legs are just right in proportion to other parts of the body. What other animals have body parts that, when they are young, seem to be considerably different than when they are adults?

3. If possible, invite a family doctor or a local health clinic worker to visit your classroom. Ask that individual to provide information on the average heights and weights of children at different ages. Students should be reminded that these measurements may be different from the heights and weights of selected individuals in the class. Invite the visitor to talk about the diet, amount of sleep, and exercise students need to maintain proper growth and development.

Art

1. Invite students to create their own "milk pictures." Have them dip toothpicks in a cup of milk and use the tips of the toothpicks to create an illustration on a sheet of paper (the toothpicks will need to be dipped several times in order to get sufficient lines of milk on the paper). Allow the milk to dry until the illustrations have disappeared (about an hour). Hold the paper next to a lightbulb and the illustrations will slowly be revealed. (The proteins in the milk become scorched when placed next to a heat source. As a result the illustration is revealed as slightly "burned" areas.)

2. Invite students to pour some whole milk into a small bowl. Carefully place four drops of four different food colors around the perimeter of the milk "pond." Carefully put a drop of liquid detergent in the middle of the pond and watch the colors begin to swirl. (The detergent "breaks up" the surface tension of the milk, causing the fat molecules to move away from each other. This movement takes the food color molecules with it, causing the swirling action.)

Math

1. Invite students to create longevity charts for various breeds of cows. Which breed lives the longest? Which breed has the shortest life span?

2. There is a recipe for an ice cream soda in chapter 8 of the book. Invite students to calculate the amount of ingredients needed to make ice cream sodas for everyone in the class. What quantities would be necessary to make enough ice cream sodas for everyone in the school? In the city?

Music

1. Invite students to create a series of sound effects that could be used along with a reading of the book. What musical instruments (real or "homemade") would create sounds of grass digesting, cows mooing, farmers milking, or babies suckling? Invite students to use common household objects (bottles, spoons, newspapers) to create appropriate sound effects.

Social Studies

1. Invite students to place a large map of the world on a bulletin board. Encourage them to write the name of each breed of cow mentioned in the book on separate index cards. They can post the cards around the map and fasten a piece of yarn from each index card to the country of origin for that breed. Which country has the most breeds?

2. Encourage students to conduct some library research on the five countries in the world with the most cows. Are those countries clustered in one or two geographical areas (the tropics, mountainous countries, etc.)? Is there a country that has more cows than people?

Physical Education

1. As part of an art activity, invite students to create a physical fitness guide for cows. What activities or exercises could cows use to stay in shape? What activities should a cow practice in order to be able to jump over the moon? The activities can be assembled into a physical fitness book for newborn cows.

The Day Jimmy's Boa Ate the Wash
Trinka Hakes Noble
New York: Dial Books for Young Readers, 1980

Summary

A boring class trip to the farm turns into an uproariously funny series of events involving cows, pigs, an egg fight, a busload of kids, and, of course, a boa constrictor.

Critical Thinking Questions

1. Why wasn't the girl very excited about the class trip?

2. What do you think the farmer and his wife will do with the boa constrictor?

3. What was the funniest part of the story? Why?

4. What do you think Jimmy will do with his new pet pig?

5. Why would your friends enjoy this book?

Reading/Language Arts

1. Encourage students to dictate or write a story called "The Day the Boa Came to Our School."

2. Students will enjoy reading other books by this author, including *Apple Tree Christmas*, *Hansy's Mermaid*, *The King's Tea*, and *Meanwhile Back at the Ranch*.

3. Invite students to write a sequel to this story, using a family pet or another familiar animal.

4. Invite each student to choose an animal to study. Students can pretend they are writing a newspaper announcement for the birth of their animal. They will need to do some research to collect necessary information. Provide the birth announcement sections of daily newspapers for students to use as a reference. Decorate a bulletin board to look like a section of a newspaper and hang the animal birth announcements there. Students can include an illustration of the new baby.

---

5. Invite each youngster to take on the role of a single animal. Encourage students to do the necessary library research on the habits and behaviors of their selected animals. Then have each student write a diary entry—as their selected animal might record it—on a day in its life.

Science/Health

1. Call the biology department of a local college or university and ask if they have any snakes on display. Find out if it would be possible for someone to visit your classroom with one or more snakes. Encourage students to create a series of questions about snakes and how they live.

2. Invite students to create several different categories for animals (e.g., mammals, reptiles, birds, etc.; scales vs. feathers; herbivores vs. carnivores; polar vs. tropical). Invite them to think of some possible rules for categorizing animals. Next have the children compare several animals; write a list on the board stating the animals' similarities and differences. Compile a list on the board on the general characteristics of each animal classification. Next, divide the students into several groups and assign an animal classification to each group. Encourage groups to record the characteristics of their animal group on a piece of poster board with magic markers. The groups can also provide five sample animals for their animal category. Invite the groups to present their findings to the class. Allow the students time to debate whether the information provided by the groups is complete and accurate. Invite student groups to develop charts explaining general information about the development of their animal classification and how that information might be shared with students in other classes.

3. Focus on a different group of animals each day, for example, insects on Monday, fish on Tuesday, carnivores on Wednesday, and so on. Each day include stories, songs, student-created plays, trivia, games, and environmental concerns related to the animal group. Invite a speaker from the community or local college to discuss current issues relating to the animals.

Art

1. Obtain some discarded pantyhose or nylon stockings. Work with students to stuff one of the legs with cloth scraps or crumpled newspaper. Paint a face on one end and turn the stocking into a replica of a boa constrictor. Retell the story and encourage students to manipulate the boa constrictor.

2. Draw the outlines of several different items of clothing (shirts, pants, shoes, etc.) on pieces of construction paper and cut them out. Tie a piece of string between two places in the classroom. Invite students to write down one important word from the story on each piece of "clothing." Use clothespins to clip the words to the string. Occasionally encourage students to use one of the words in an original sentence.

Math

1. Encourage students to keep an animal journal of all the animals they see during the week. They should include pets, wild animals, insects, and animals seen on television or outside. Hang charts for mammals, fish, birds, reptiles and amphibians, and so on. Students can add to the charts daily. Which group of animals has the highest number?

Music

1. Provide students with an inexpensive tape recorder that has a microphone attached by a cord. Invite them to tape the microphone handle to the end of a broom handle or long pole (be sure no tape covers the microphone itself). Encourage students to go outside on a clear and calm day (no wind blowing, for example) and place the microphone near one or more wildlife homes (e.g., a bird's nest, a beehive, a wasp's nest [Be Careful!]). The students should check first to be sure the animal(s) are home. Invite them to record and catalog various animal sounds.

Social Studies

1. Have a class pet show. Invite each student to sign up for a time slot to show his or her pet. If some students do not own pets, invite them to make a presentation on a pet they would like to own, or to adopt a pet from a friend or neighbor for the day. Plan time to talk with students about the role or value of pets in the life of a family.

2. Arrange for the local SPCA (Society for the Prevention of Cruelty to Animals) to give a presentation on pet care, adopting pets, and birth control for pets. How does pet ownership affect the local community? What is the role of other animals in the life of the community?

Physical Education

1. Invite children to make a large chart (on an oversized piece of poster board, for example) that lists the speeds at which animals in the book travel. The chart can order animals from the fastest to the slowest or vice versa. How much faster is their pet than the slowest animal on the chart? How much slower is the family dog than the fastest animal on the chart? Where would students place themselves on the chart? What physical activities would they need to practice to maintain their speed?

Dinosaurs: Strange and Wonderful
Laurence Pringle
Honesdale, PA: Boyds Mills Press, 1995

Summary

A detailed and fascinating overview of some of the most well-known dinosaurs, how they lived and died, and how scientists have learned about these "terrible lizards." Information on dinosaur habits and the work of paleontologists highlight this book.

Critical Thinking Questions

1. What is the most interesting fact you know about dinosaurs?

2. What do you think would be the most interesting part of a paleontologist's job?

3. Which dinosaur is your favorite? What habits or physical characteristics make it your favorite?

4. What do you think is the greatest mystery surrounding dinosaurs? How do you think scientists will solve that mystery?

Reading/Language Arts

1. If you live near a college or university, call the biology department, zoology department, or archaeology department and ask to speak to a "dinosaur expert." Set up a person-to-person interview with a professor and the students. Invite students to assemble a list of questions prior to the visit. Most scientists are eager to share information with youngsters and can offer some important information concerning recent discoveries. The institution may also have some fossils or bones to share with students.

2. Several commercial companies sell authentic fossils or replicas of fossils. Invite students to write to some of these companies and ask for a current catalog. When the catalogs arrive, invite students to read them and note the types of materials offered by each company. You may wish to order one or more fossils or dinosaur eggs from these companies. Here are a few to get you started (listings of others can be found in the back pages of *Earth* magazine): Phoenix Fossils (6401 E. Camino de Los Ranchos, Scottsdale, AZ 85254); Older Than Dirt (P.O. Box 371, Moorpark, CA 93020); and Natural History Supply House (12419 Coronet Dr., Sun City West, AZ 85375).

3. Invite students to put together a "dinosaur newspaper" (in a newspaper format) that presents interesting facts and observations about dinosaurs. Invite them to use the same sections as the local newspaper (sports—how fast some dinosaurs were able to run; fashion—speculation on the colors of various dinosaurs; food and health—the different diets of meat-eaters and plant-eaters). Students can use a word processing program to assemble the newspaper and then print it for distribution to other classrooms.

4. Here are some other books students may enjoy reading on their own: *Bones, Bones, Dinosaur Bones* by Byron Barton (New York: HarperCollins, 1990); *Dinosaur Dinners* by Sharon Cosner (New York: Watts, 1991); *How Did Dinosaurs Live?* by Hisa Kunihiko (Minneapolis, MN: Lerner, 1990); *Discovering Dinosaur Babies* by Miriam Schlein (New York: Four Winds, 1991); and *Dinosaurs* by John Wexo (Mankato, MN: Creative Educations, 1991).

5. Here are two books of dinosaur poetry that students will definitely enjoy: *Dinosaurs* by Lee Bennett Hopkins (San Diego, CA: Harcourt Brace, 1987) and *Tyrannosaurus Was a Beast* by Jack Prelutsky (New York: Greenwillow Books, 1988).

Science/Health

1. The following activity will demonstrate some of the difficulties scientists face when attempting to reconstruct a dinosaur skeleton (or a portion of a skeleton):

   Place a whole (unboned) chicken in a pot of water to which has been added one or two cups of vinegar. Boil the chicken completely (until the meat almost falls off the skeleton). Remove as much meat as possible and continue to boil until all the meat can be removed with your hands. (CAREFUL: The meat will be hot.) Allow the chicken skeleton to cool completely and then carefully separate the individual bones. Allow the bones to dry in the open for about two to three days.

Provide students with the pile of bones and invite them to reconstruct the entire chicken skeleton according to what they know a chicken looks like. (NOTE: Inform students that they may have difficulty in reassembling the chicken skeleton even though they may have seen live chickens or illustrations of chickens. Invite them to imagine the difficulties of scientists reassembling a dinosaur skeleton [or part of one] when nobody has ever seen a live dinosaur.)

Art

1. Different artists have illustrated dinosaurs in different ways throughout the years. The most famous dinosaur of all—Tyrannosaurus Rex—has been depicted by various artists as slow and dumb or as cunning and fast.

   Invite students to assemble a collection of drawings and illustrations of selected dinosaurs for display. They may wish to search through encyclopedias, different trade books on dinosaurs, or scientific magazines for different renditions of identical dinosaurs. Invite students to discuss some of the reasons different artists have depicted the same dinosaur in various ways. What are some of the similarities? What are some of the differences?

Math

1. Dinosaurs came in all shapes and sizes. Students are sometimes amazed at the heights, weights, and lengths of some of the more popular dinosaurs. However, in order to fully appreciate dinosaurs' sizes they need a frame of reference or a comparison feature. Here's one way to help students appreciate how huge these animals were.

   Measure various lengths of string, twine, or yarn according to the following measurements. Go to a driveway or the school playground and lay out several pieces of string side by side. Invite students to mark the ends of each piece of string with chalk. Encourage youngsters to compare the distances by lying down next to them, walking them off with their feet, or some other comparable form of measurement.

Dinosaur	*Length*
Compsognathus	2 feet
Velociraptor	8 feet
Stegosaurus	28 feet
Triceratops	30 feet
Tyrannosaurus Rex	32 feet
Brachiosaurus	67 feet
Ultrasaurus	100 feet

   Afterward, invite students to make a list of objects with which they are very familiar (school bus, automobile, house) and develop a chart that compares dinosaur lengths with familiar objects in their environment.

Music

1. Invite students to create their own dinosaur songs using the music from another song. For example, here is a song that can be sung to the tune of "I've Been Working on the Railroad":

> I've been watching Stegosaurus
> All the livelong day
> I've been watching Stegosaurus
> Just to see what he would say
> Can't you hear him munchin', crunchin'
> Rise up and start to eat a tree
> Don't you ever want to meet him
> 'Cause he will make you flee.

Social Studies

1. Dinosaurs have been discovered in many states throughout the United States. Provide students with a list of those states (following) and encourage them to locate information in trade books or library references listing representative examples of uncovered dinosaurs in each state. Students can post illustrations of those dinosaurs around a wall map of the United States with a length of yarn tacked to the picture at one end and to the indicated state at the other end. States where dinosaurs have been discovered: Alabama, Alaska, Arizona, Arkansas, Colorado, Connecticut, Kansas, Maryland, Massachusetts, Michigan, Mississippi, Missouri, Montana, New Jersey, New Mexico, North Carolina, Oklahoma, South Dakota, Texas, Utah, and Wyoming.

Physical Education

1. Schedule a "dinosaur-walk relay." Post a list of dinosaurs on the chalkboard and invite the class to assemble into two teams. The first member of each team must imitate the walk of the first dinosaur. The second member of each team must imitate the walk of the second dinosaur, and so on (practice sessions may be needed beforehand). The first team to complete the list is the winner. Examples of some dinosaurs to include are: *Velociraptor*, *Triceratops*, *Stegosaurus*, *Brachiosaurus*, and *Ultrasaurus*.

The Flunking of Joshua T. Bates
Susan Shreve
New York: Borzoi Books, 1984

Summary

On his way home from the beach, Joshua T. Bates receives the news that he must repeat third grade. With the help of a kind teacher, Joshua tries to work his way to fourth grade. Although he is teased by some of his old classmates, he gets the last laugh.

Critical Thinking Questions

1. Why is it important for children to learn how to read? What might be some consequences if students did not learn how to read in school?

2. If you were Joshua, how would you have handled some of the situations he found himself in during the story? Would you have behaved any differently?

3. What do you think Joshua would have done if he had not passed his test? How would he have felt?

4. Can you define the word *friendship*? What does a friend mean to you? How important are friends?

5. If you could, what would you like to tell the author of this story?

6. Do you know anyone similar to Joshua? Describe that individual.

Reading/Language Arts

1. Invite individual students to select one of the characters in the story and write a series of diary entries through the eyes of that character. How did that character feel about the other characters in the story? How did it feel to beat the fourth-graders in softball?

2. Make arrangements with a colleague in a grade lower than yours to set up a tutoring bureau in which several of your students work with the younger students. The tutoring can consist of practicing math facts, reading stories, or working on a science project. The tutors should maintain journals about their experiences to discuss in class at a later time.

3. Divide the class into several groups and encourage each group to talk about what Joshua's friend should have done. Have each group share its decision(s) with the rest of the class. Did Joshua's friend make the right decision to talk to Joshua only when nobody else was looking?

---

4. Encourage students to write an imaginary letter to Joshua just after he finds out he will be repeating third grade. What should they say to him? How can they comfort him? Can they suggest something to help him deal with the situation? Have they ever been involved in a similar experience?

5. Invite students to participate in a panel discussion on the pros and cons of repeating a grade. What benefits are there for the students? Do those benefits outweigh the negative emotions of the situation? How should students react? How should parents react? Perhaps students can come up with some guidelines or suggestions and put them in a flyer to distribute through the guidance counselor's office (you may wish to invite the guidance counselor to your class for a series of interviews).

Science/Health

1. Students may be interested in observing birds. Cut part of the side out of a milk container and fill the bottom with bird seed. Hang the feeder outside your classroom window. Instruct students to observe and record the types of birds that visit the feeder, when they come, how many use it, and the amount of feed consumed. The feeder and records can be maintained for an extended period of time throughout the school year. An excellent book on the subject is *Backyard Bird Watching* by George H. Harrison (Minocqua, WI: Willow Creek Press, 1997).

2. Bring in an old aquarium and have students establish a terrarium that depicts the flora of a particular region of Africa. What kinds of plants, rocks, wood, and so on can they place in the terrarium so that it accurately represents a region of Africa (library research may be necessary before beginning this project). If you're interested in obtaining a free catalog of animal "containers" including cages, aquariums, terrariums, and birdhouses, write to Martin's Aquarium (101 Old York Rd., Rt. 611, Jenkintown, PA 19046).

3. Invite the school nurse to visit and discuss common childhood injuries. He or she can explain how to prevent and treat these injuries and perhaps demonstrate simple first aid procedures.

4. The National Geographic Society (Washington, DC) has a variety of intriguing videos on the richness and vastness of the African continent. Try to obtain one or more of the following for your students: *Africa* (no. 51440), *Journey to the Forgotten River* (no. 51461), *Serengeti Diary* (no. 51388), *African Odyssey* (no. 51336), *Bushmen of the Kalahari* (no. 51027), *African Wildlife* (no. 50509), *Africa's Stolen River* (no. 51373), and *Lions of the African Night* (no. 51331).

Art

1. Provide students with index cards and invite them to design postcards that could be sent from Africa to a friend living in the United States. What illustration(s) could be used for the cards? Have students collect these postcards and display them on the bulletin board. Your students will want to consult some of the following resource books: *In Africa* by Marc Bernheim (New York: Atheneum, 1973); *A Is for Africa* by Jean Bond (New York: Watts, 1969); *Wild Animals of Africa* by Beatrice Borden (New York: Random House, 1982); *Jambo Means Hello* by Muriel Feelings (New York: Dial Books for Young Readers, 1974); and *Ashanti to Zulu* by Margaret Musgrove (New York: Dial Books for Young Readers, 1976).

2. Invite students to create a new book cover or dust jacket for the book. Encourage them to fold and illustrate sheets of construction paper with a drawing or portrait of Joshua or his classmates. Students can be encouraged to illustrate a representational scene from the book to entice a potential reader.

3. Students may enjoy creating a "shoe box jungle." Invite students to bring in toy animals or create their own out of modeling clay. They can create trees and bushes out of construction paper or with leaves and twigs found around school.

Math

1. Demonstrate to students how to compute batting averages (number of hits divided by the number of times at bat). Provide them with some examples of batting averages from the local newspaper. Encourage students to play one or more games of softball and then compute their individual batting averages (the emphasis is on math, not on who has the highest average!).

2. Involve students in computing their grades for portions of a course or for a selected series of tests or quizzes. You may elect to have students use calculators or a preferred computer program to determine their respective grades. Encourage them to keep track of their grades (show them your grade book, for example) for a period of time.

3. Invite students to compute distances from your school to various locations in Africa. Later, they may wish to calculate the travel time to those locations via different vehicles (airplane flying at 450 mph, boat traveling at 12 mph, car going at 50 mph, etc.).

4. Encourage students to construct simple clocks from paper plates and cardboard hands. Ask them to each select a city in Africa and determine the time in that city (in comparison with the time in your specific time zone). Ask students to adjust their clocks to the correct time.

Music

1. Students may enjoy listening to true African music. Check with your local public library for recordings of African music that you can play for your students. One resource is *African Musical Instruments* with Bilal Abdurahuram, arranged by Ayyub Addullah (New York: Asch Records). Another is *The Music of Africa Series: Uganda 1* by Hugh Tracey (Washington, DC: Traditional Music Documentation Project, 1972 [LP]).

2. Contact Folkways Records (New York) and ask for a copy of the current catalog (the school's music teacher may have a copy). This company has one of the most extensive collections of authentic and traditional music from many lands. Obtain one or more recordings to share with your students.

Social Studies

1. Invite small groups of students to construct travel guides or maps of how Joshua could get to Africa. Encourage students to plan several itineraries and travel routes based on sites to see, cost, and time of year.

2. Invite students to interview their grandparents or older citizens in their neighborhood on how "flunking" was handled in their day. Were students retained as much then as they are now or did they just drop out of school? What kinds of counseling services were available to help youngsters deal with the difficulty of repeating a grade? Did they ever repeat a grade; if so, how did they feel about it?

3. Students may wish to correspond with African pen pals through the Afro-Asian Center (P.O. Box 337, Saugerties, NY 12477 [914-246-7828]).

4. Have an African food celebration. Bring in a variety of foods native to Africa: honey, dates, coffee, cloves (try clove gum), yams, sunflower seeds, peanuts, grapes, and olives. Invite students to each write a paragraph describing their reactions to the foods.

Physical Education

1. Invite students to set up and carry out a bike rally. What kinds of events would be appropriate (obstacle course, straight races, closed course for time, etc.). Students may wish to invent many different events.

2. Take students on a long walk in the neighborhood or around the school grounds. Invite them to pretend they are on a safari in Africa.

3. Your class may wish to set up a softball tournament with other classes. Decide how many games each team will play and how to decide on the tournament victor. As part of an art activity, invite students to design and construct appropriate awards or ribbons for the winners.

Ira Sleeps Over
Bernard Waber
Boston: Houghton Mifflin, 1972

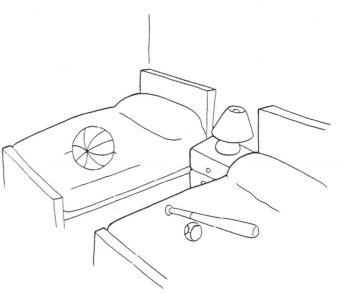

Summary

Ira's friend invites him to sleep over. Ira has one small problem—should he bring his teddy bear along? Ira discovers that he isn't the only one with a teddy bear.

Critical Thinking Questions

1. How would the story have been different if Reggie did not have a teddy bear?

2. Where do you think Reggie and Ira got the names for their teddy bears?

3. Why do you think Ira's sister made so much fun of him?

4. If you spent the night at a friend's house what would you want to do for fun?

Reading/Language Arts

1. Invite students to create a written or oral story from the perspective of Tah-Tah. Do they think Tah-Tah might have felt neglected?

2. Invite students to pretend they are news reporters for a local television station. Encourage them to make up a series of questions they would like to ask Ira. You can take on the role of Ira and respond to the questions students ask.

3. Talk with students about some of their bedtime routines (watch TV, take a bath, put pajamas on, say goodnight to parents, etc.). Invite students to make a list of bedtime routines shared by members of the class.

4. Encourage students to write an invitation to Ira to sleep at their homes. Have them include all of the activities planned.

5. Discuss with students the funniest, the scariest, the darkest, or the noisiest place they have ever slept. What is the most comfortable place they have slept in? Invite students to construct a class book that records their thoughts and ideas.

Science/Health

1. Talk with students about babies' and toddlers' need for naps and what happens when they don't nap. Why is it important for growing babies to get lots of sleep? If possible, invite a doctor or the school nurse to visit your classroom to discuss the importance of sleep in a growing person's life.

2. The three major health needs for growing children are a nutritious diet, regular exercise, and sufficient sleep. Invite students to make a personal notebook divided into three sections. In the first section, each student can record the foods he or she eats (even snacks) during the course of a week. Students may want to divide a sheet of paper into the four major food groups (vegetable-fruit group; bread-cereal group; meat-poultry-fish-bean group; and milk-cheese group) and record the types and amounts of each eaten during the week. In the exercise section, each youngster can record the type and duration of various physical activities he or she participates in during the week. In the third section, each student can record the number of hours of sleep he or she gets each night of the selected week. Invite students to share their notebooks with a family doctor for comments and suggestions.

Art

1. Invite students to create bear collages by cutting pictures of various bears from old magazines. After the pictures are cut, encourage students to paste the pictures onto large pieces of paper.

2. Encourage students to make puppets using old socks, pieces of cloth, yarn, glue, and buttons or sequins (for eyes, mouth, buttons on shirt, etc.). Retell the story, providing opportunities for students to use the puppets during selected scenes.

Math

1. The average adult needs approximately eight hours of sleep a night. The average child needs approximately 10 hours of sleep a night. The average baby sleeps about 14–16 hours a day. At that rate, how many hours (approximately) has a 10-year-old slept since birth? A 21-year-old? A 65-year-old?

2. Invite students to make charts and graphs of the sleep habits of members of their families. They may wish to record information such as who sleeps the longest, who sleeps the least, and what is the longest anyone has slept undisturbed.

Music

1. Invite students to work with the school's music teacher to assemble a collection of bedtime music or lullabies. What traditional songs or tunes can they include in the collection? Plan time for students to talk about why these songs were created for young children.

Social Studies

1. Students may be interested in conducting some library research on the sleeping customs or habits of different peoples around the world. How do children in other countries prepare for bed? Students may wish to put together an informational book illustrating some of those routines.

Physical Education

1. Invite students to set up and carry out a bicycle rally. What kinds of events would be appropriate (obstacle courses, straight races, closed course for time, etc.)? Encourage students to invent as many different events as possible.

Miss Nelson Is Missing!
Harry Allard
Boston: Houghton Mifflin, 1977

Summary

The students of Room 207 were the most misbehaved in the school. Miss Nelson, their teacher, suddenly disappeared, and Miss Viola Swamp arrived with hours of homework. The class tries to figure out what happened to Miss Nelson.

Critical Thinking Questions

1. When you had a substitute, how was she similar to Miss Swamp? How was your substitute different?

2. Would you want to have Miss Nelson as a teacher?

3. How would you feel about having a substitute teacher like Viola Swamp?

4. If you were Detective McSmogg, where would you have started looking for Miss Nelson? Why?

5. How would you have felt if you were one of the students when Miss Nelson returned? Why?

Reading/Language Arts

1. Talk with students about some of the qualities of a good teacher. What should good teachers do? How should they act toward their students? How should they teach? Invite students to assemble their data in the form of a brochure or leaflet that can be shared with the principal, superintendent, or school board.

2. Encourage students to dictate or write a sequel to the story. Have Detective McSmogg looking for Miss Viola Swamp. Where would he look for her? Would he ever find her? The sequels can be printed via a word processor and donated to the school library.

---

3. Students will enjoy reading the two sequels to this story, *Miss Nelson Is Back* and *Miss Nelson Has a Field Day.*

4. Invite students to write a letter to Miss Nelson asking her to come back to the classroom. What would students want to say to convince Miss Nelson that she should return?

Science/Health

1. Invite students to create their own homemade gliders with the following activity: Cut two 2-inch strips (lengthwise) from an index card. Form each of the two strips into loops (one loop should be considerably smaller than the other). Secure each loop with a paper clip. Slip the paper clip fastened to one loop over the end of a drinking straw. Slip the other loop in the same way over the other end of the straw. Using the small loop as the front of the toy, students can throw the invention in the air and watch it glide (this may take a little practice to perfect). If appropriate, explain Bernoulli's principle (why objects such as birds, airplanes, and gliders tend to stay aloft) to students. Provide opportunities for students to decorate their homemade gliders.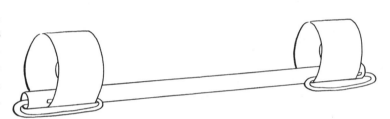

Art

1. Invite students to make a wanted poster for Miss Nelson. What kind of information should be included on the poster? Post the finished poster in the hallway outside your classroom or in the main office.

2. Students may also wish to create a wanted poster for Miss Viola Swamp. How would the two wanted posters differ? How would they be the same?

3. The classroom illustrated in the book had no distinguishing features. Invite students to design the perfect classroom. What features or characteristics should it have? What are the major differences between the students' classroom, the classroom in the book, and their ideal classroom?

Math

1. In Miss Nelson's class, the students always refused to do their homework. Invite your students to create a homework assignment in math that would be particularly appropriate (and very exciting) for other students at your grade level. What considerations need to be kept in mind in designing a math assignment? How does a math homework assignment differ from assignments in other areas? What difficulties do students have in designing an assignment?

Music

1. Invite students to create a class song that reflects their activities and group spirit. Provide them with examples of songs at various colleges and local high schools (e.g., football fight songs).

Social Studies

1. Invite students to look through several old magazines and cut out pictures of children they would like to have in their classroom. Encourage students to paste these pictures on a large sheet of paper. Talk about why the selected children would be welcome in their class.

2. Students may be interested in designing an application form for substitute teachers. The following is one they may wish to modify or alter:

Name: _____

Address: _____

_____

Position applied for: _____

Work experience: _____

_____

Training/education: _____

_____

Special qualifications: _____

_____

Awards/certificates: _____

_____

References: _____

_____

After students have created their own form, invite them to share it with the school principal. Students may want to obtain a copy of the school or district application form for substitute teachers and compare it with their final form.

Physical Education

1. Invite students to play several team sports (e.g., softball, basketball). Discuss with them the similarities between a team working together and a class of students and a teacher working together. What are some of the advantages of group work? How does teamwork help a group achieve its goals?

The Salamander Room
Anne Mazer
New York: Knopf, 1991

Summary

A young boy discovers a little orange salamander in the woods and takes it home. Prodded by a series of questions from his mother, he thinks of all the imaginative ways he will care for his newfound friend and how his companion will live.

Critical Thinking Questions

1. What are some things you must think about when caring for an animal?

2. If you could choose any pet in the world, what would you have?

3. If you could add a sequel to this story, what would you say?

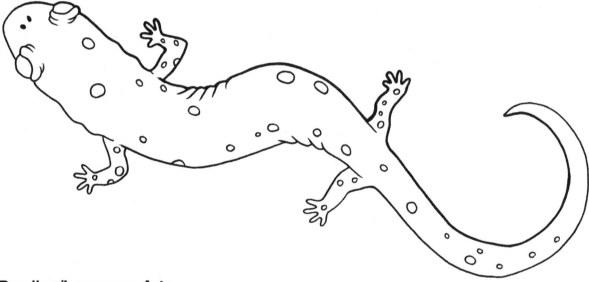

Reading/Language Arts

1. Invite students to research other books on salamanders. Encourage them to collect additional data about the lifestyles and habits of different species of salamanders. What are some of the similarities? What are some of the differences? Students may wish to assemble their data into an informative book, video, or hypertext presentation.

2. Invite students to rewrite a portion of the story from the perspective of the salamander. What did it observe and experience? How did the salamander view the little boy? What did it think about living in the little boy's bedroom?

3. In this activity—known as "word addition"—students add poetic phrases to factual details or vice versa to create "arithmetic with words." For example,

    leaves that are fresh and green + moss that looks like little stars = a salamander bed

---

In the example above students used the book's phrases "leaves that are fresh and green" and "moss that looks like little stars" and created their own sum—"a salamander bed."

warm and cozy + little and orange = a salamander

Invite students to add their own phrases to favorite phrases from the book and create their own word-addition "problems." Students may wish to begin by "adding" only two phrases and progress to the "addition" of three or four that "equal" another phrase from the book or one they have made up.

Provide opportunities for students to share their word-addition problems with others by collecting them into a notebook or by posting them on a large wall chart. Students may also wish to trace and cut out an oversized outline of a salamander from poster board and print their word-addition problems across the face of this poster.

Science/Health

1. Contact a zoologist or herpetologist at the biology or zoology department of a local college or university. If possible, make arrangements for that individual to visit your classroom so that students have opportunities to talk with him or her and ask questions.

2. Invite youngsters to keep a journal of the activities, habits, travels, and motions of a single animal. Kids may want to select a house pet or some other animal they can observe regularly throughout the day. Provide youngsters with a field journal—a simple notebook wildlife biologists frequently use to track the activities of one or more wild animals over the course of an extended period of time.

   Have students include in the notebook brief "field notes" on what the animal did; how it behaved; what it ate; how it acted in the presence of other animals, including its own kind; if and when it slept; and how it moved about in its environment. If, for example, a student selects the family dog, he or she can note when and where it eats, where it relieves itself, when and at whom it barks, the positions in which it sleeps, and the specific places it travels in and outside the house. Students may also want to include some illustrations in their field journals.

   Point out to youngsters that when they observe quite closely the habits and behaviors of an animal they are familiar with, they may discover some interesting details they were not aware of. Plan time to discuss with youngsters the new information they learned in their "field observations." How does that information compare with their previous impressions?

Art

1. The illustrations in this book are striking and colorful. They are an important part of the story line and add immeasurably to the "tone" of the story. Invite students to look through other examples of children's books about animals to note how well the illustrations match the text. To start, students may wish to look at examples of children's books published 25 years or more ago and compare those with books published in the past two or three years. Plan time to discuss differences between "old" books and more recent children's books.

2. Invite students to create a forest environment in the classroom. Cover the walls with paper and encourage students to paint scenes of a forest, using vibrant colors. Individual animals can be painted directly on the paper or created out of papier-mâché or cardboard and suspended from the ceiling with strings. Make some of the trees and plants in relief by constructing them out of cardboard and attaching them so they stand out from the wall.

Math

1. The book tells about many growing things such as trees, mushrooms, and ferns. Invite students to select several plants outside the classroom or on the school grounds and measure them in various ways (i.e., height, length of leaves, width of trunk or stalk, diameter of flowers, etc.). Encourage students to keep charts or graphs of their measurements over an extended period of time (e.g., three months, six months). Invite students to discuss those plants that seem to have faster and slower rates of growth. They can assemble their information in a descriptive brochure or booklet.

2. Encourage students to conduct some library research on the growth rates of various species of salamanders. For example, does a red eft salamander (the type depicted in the book) grow faster or slower than a tiger salamander or spotted salamander? Invite students to create appropriate graphs of their collected research.

3. Bring in a cross section of a tree trunk. Show students how to count the rings in order to tell the age of the tree. Invite students to count the rings to come up with an approximate date for the tree's "birthday." Students may wish to repeat this activity with other tree samples.

Music

1. This book is a celebration of nature and the positive relationships between humans and animals. Invite students to listen to some environmental music (prerecorded tapes are available from The Nature Company, P.O. Box 188, Florence, KY 41022 [1-800-227-1114] and NorthSound, P.O. Box 1360, Minocqua, WI 54548 [1-800-336-6398]). Encourage students to discuss the relationships between the background sounds of nature on those tapes and the accompanying music. Which of the tapes would provide appropriate music for a telling of *The Salamander Room*?

Social Studies

1. Invite students to imagine that they are the tiny salamander in the story. Encourage them to talk about their home, their environment, and their ecosystem. What is so special about the place they live? How is their particular location similar to or different from Brian's? What qualities are required in every home in order to make it livable (for either a human or an animal)?

2. Provide students with blank maps and invite them to color in the places in your county, state, or region in which salamanders can be found. Which areas seem to have the greatest varieties of salamanders? Which areas have the fewest species?

Physical Education

1. Introduce the art of mime to your students. Invite students to go through the motions associated with various activities (e.g., raking leaves, setting the table, cooking, playing football). They can also form groups and pantomime various types of classroom activities (e.g., going to lunch, getting ready for the school bus, etc.). Afterward, encourage small groups of students to create special mime routines for selected sections of this book. Emphasize to students that mime is much more than doing an activity without speaking—it is also a form of expression through control of muscles and body movements. If possible, contact a local theater group to demonstrate some techniques to your students.

GRADE 4

Cloudy with a Chance of Meatballs
Judi Barrett
New York: Macmillan, 1978

Summary

In the land of Chewandswallow the weather brings showers of food and drink for the people three times a day. One day the weather gets out of control, raining massive quantities of food, and forces the people of Chewandswallow to find a new land to call their home.

Critical Thinking Questions

1. How would you feel if you didn't have a choice of what to eat for breakfast, lunch, and dinner?

2. What would it be like to be forced to leave your country and start all over in a strange land?

3. How do you think the people of Chewandswallow felt when they moved to the new land and had to go shopping for their food?

4. If you had to leave the country right now, what would you take with you? Why?

Reading/Language Arts

1. Here are some excellent weather books for students to read and share: *What Will the Weather Be?* by Linda DeWitt (New York: HarperCollins, 1991); *Weather Words and What They Mean* by Gail Gibbons (New York: Holiday House, 1990); *Nature All Year Long* by Clare Leslie (New York: Greenwillow Books, 1991); *A Rainy Day* by Sandra Markle (New York: Orchard, 1993); and *The Weather Sky* by Bruce McMillan (New York: Farrar, Straus & Giroux, 1991).

2. Invite students to gather newspaper and magazine articles about weather or bring in daily weather forecasts from local newspapers or TV news shows. Articles can be filed in shoeboxes and shared in a "weather news" area. Encourage students to examine all of the clippings and compile a list comparing and contrasting the different types of forecasts.

3. Before reading *Cloudy with a Chance of Meatballs*, invite students to form their chairs in a circle. Go around the circle and encourage each student to create a wild and wacky form of weather (e.g., "The sun was like a melted lump of butter," "Rain came down like spraying soda pop," and "The snow was like huge mountains of mashed potatoes"). Write the statements on sheets of construction paper and post them on the bulletin board.

4. After listening to several sample statements (in the previous activity), invite each student to select one and write a tall tale in his or her journal. These tales may be illustrated and posted if desired.

Science/Health

1. Talk with students about the four major food groups (milk and eggs, fruit and vegetables, grain and bread, meat and fish). Invite students to list the titles of each of the four groups at the top of a large sheet of paper. Encourage them to list foods from the book in the proper food group. Which food group has the most items? Do the people of Chewandswallow eat balanced meals? What must be done to make sure their diet is balanced?

2. Invite children to create their own homemade weather station. The following instruments will help them learn about the weather and some of the ways meteorologists measure various aspects of the weather.

   a. *Thermometer.* Use a nail to dig out a hole in the center of a small cork. Fill a bottle to the brim with colored water and push the cork into the neck of the bottle. Push a straw into the hole in the center of the cork. Mark the line the water rises to in the straw with a felt-tip pen. Note the temperature on a regular thermometer and mark that on a narrow strip of paper glued next to the straw. Take measurements on several days, noting the temperature on a regular thermometer and marking that at the spot where the water rises in the straw on the strip of paper. After several readings, youngsters will have a fairly accurate thermometer. (Liquids expand when heated [water rises in the straw] and contract when cooled [water lowers in the straw].)

b. *Barometer.* Stretch a balloon over the top of a wide-mouth jar and secure it with a rubber band. Glue a straw horizontally on top of the stretched balloon, starting from the center of the balloon (the straw should extend beyond the edge of the jar). Attach a pin horizontally to the end of the straw. Place another straw in a spool and attach an index card to the end. Place this device next to the jar so that the pin is close to and points to the index card. (When air pressure increases, the pressure

inside the bottle is less than that of the outside air. Therefore, the balloon rubber pushes down, and the pointer end of the straw moves up [that spot can be marked on the index card]. When the air pressure goes down, the air inside the jar presses harder than the outside air. The rubber pushes up and tightens, and the pointer moves down. Point out to children that when the pointer moves down, bad weather is probably on the way because air pressure falls when a storm is approaching. When the pointer rises, that's usually a sign that good weather is on the way.)

c. *Anemometer.* Cut out two strips of cardboard approximately 2 x 16 inches. Make a slit in the middle of each one so they fit together to make an X. Cut four

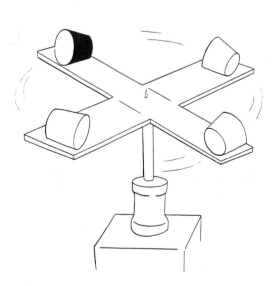

small paper cups so they are all about one-inch high. Staple the bottom of each cup to one "arm" of the X. Use a felt-tipped marker to color one of the cups. Make a hole in the center of the X with a needle.

Stick the eye of a needle into the eraser of a pencil and place the pencil into a spool (jam some paper around the sides of the spool hole so that the pencil stays erect). Glue the spool to a large block of wood. Place the X on the tip of the needle so that it twirls around freely. Blow on the cups to make sure they spin around freely (some adjustments on the size of the hole may need to be made). Invite youngsters to place their anemometer outside on a breezy day and count the number of times the colored cup spins past a certain point. That will give them a rough idea of wind speed. (Meteorologists use a device similar to this one, but the revolutions are

From *The Integrated Curriculum, Second Edition.* © 1998 Anthony D. Fredericks. Teacher Ideas Press. (800) 237-6124.

counted electronically.) Later, you may wish to introduce youngsters to the Beaufort scale—a widely used scale to judge the speed of wind.

Children may wish to set up their makeshift weather station outside and take regular "readings." They can compare their measurements with those in the daily newspaper. Children should record their readings over a period of several days or weeks in a journal or appropriate notebook.

3. Many strange things have fallen from the sky as a result of unusual weather patterns. Students may want to research some of these unusual events and assemble them together into a notebook entitled "Weird and Wacky Weather." Here are a few to get them started:

    a. On October 14, 1755, red snow fell on the Alps.

    b. In June 1940 a shower of silver coins fell on the town of Gorky, Russia.

    c. On June 16, 1939, it rained frogs at Trowbridge, England.

Art

1. If possible, invite selected students to take photographs of various cloud patterns. When the photos are developed ask students to arrange them into an attractive display for the entire class. Students may wish to include descriptions of each cloud type and what it means in terms of impending weather.

Math

1. If possible, take students on a field trip to the local supermarket. Invite them to locate the prices of all the foods mentioned in the story. Encourage them to figure out the cost of a sample meal as illustrated in the book. They can also figure out what it might cost to make a dinner of their choice.

2. Invite students to complete a temperature chart. Encourage them to work in groups of two or three as follows:

    a. Place a thermometer outside in a shady area.

    b. Note the temperature in the morning, at noon, and in the afternoon on each of several days.

    c. Put three dots on a graph to indicate the temperatures measured for that day. Connect the dots to illustrate the rise and fall in daily temperature.

    d. Keep an ongoing record of daily temperatures over a span of several weeks (the temperature charts can be posted on a bulletin board or collected into a scrapbook).

Music

1. Invite each student to imagine that he or she is a particular form of weather (a raindrop, a gust of wind, a snowflake, etc.). Encourage students to write about their "life cycle" from the perspective of that particular form of weather. What are some of the things observed? What distances are traveled? How long is the life span? Encourage students to "score" their form of weather by matching it to a popular song or melody. For example, what type of music could be matched with falling rain?

Social Studies

1. In the story, there is a newspaper with current events. Invite students to make a "food newspaper" about food, cooking, meals, and other eating events that take place at home. How can dinner be turned into a sporting event? How can breakfast be turned into front-page news? How can lunch be developed into a business section?

2. Discuss why weather is different in different places. How can we find out the weather in the United States? What symbols could we use to record and report the weather on a map? Use the map in your local newspaper to find out this information. For homework, have students find out about the weather patterns in the United States. Make weather symbols from pieces of construction paper and position them on a map of the United States to denote the weather forecast for that particular day. Change these as the conditions in selected areas change.

3. Many sayings and predictions about the weather have been handed down from one generation to the next. Following are two sayings or admonitions that have been passed down through the years:

   a. Red sky at morning—sailor take warning. Red sky at night—sailor's delight.
   b. A January fog will freeze a hog.

   Invite students to look through other books and assemble a collection of weather sayings that have been handed down through the years. How accurate are those sayings? How do those sayings compare with actual meteorological events?

4. People did not always understand the weather; they had many beliefs about the causes of weather patterns. Following are a few:

   a. Sea fog was once thought to be the breath of an underwater monster.
   b. In Germany, some people believed that a cat washes itself just before a rain shower.
   c. The Aztecs believed that the sun god could be kept strong and bright only through human sacrifices.
   d. The Norse thought that weather was created by the god Thor, who raced across the sky in a chariot pulled by two giant goats.

   Invite students to research other beliefs people had about the weather. They may wish to collect their data from trade books, encyclopedias, or conversations with weather experts. Encourage them to collect these beliefs into a notebook or journal.

5. Obtain a copy of *USA Today*. Show students the color weather map on the back of the first section. Invite them to note the various designations used to record weather information. Encourage them to read through the weather section and note the predictions for their area of the country. They can create a special weather map similar to the one in *USA Today*, but specifically tailored for their geographic region (as opposed to the entire United States).

Physical Education

1. Create a treasure map (with various food items selected from the book as the treasure). Encourage students to go through an obstacle course to locate the hidden treasure.

East of the Sun and West of the Moon
Mercer Mayer
New York: Macmillan, 1980

Summary

The beautiful daughter of a farmer and his wife faces hardship when her father becomes ill and she must seek water from the South Wind. A frog assists her in return for three wishes. When the frog wishes to marry her, she refuses and kills him. A spell is broken and the frog turns into a handsome youth who is taken away to the Land of East of the Sun and West of the Moon to wed the Troll Princess. The maiden travels in search of her love with the help of enchanting creatures along the way.

Critical Thinking Questions

1. What would have happened if the maiden had turned into a frog? What would the youth have done?

2. What would you do if a frog asked you to marry him? Would you react in the same way the maiden did?

3. The frog was to ask for three wishes, but asked for only two. What would have been the third wish?

4. How would the story have been different if the youth wasn't a frog but another animal such as a cat, rabbit, or giraffe?

5. Where is the Land of East of the Sun and West of the Moon?

6. Is it always important to keep a promise? Why or why not?

Reading/Language Arts

1. Call your local public library and make arrangements for a storyteller to visit your classroom (your local yellow pages may also list a storytelling guild in your area). Have the storyteller share stories in the same genre as "East of the Sun . . . ."

2. To reinforce how folktales are passed down from generation to generation, divide the class into several groups and direct each group to create its own original folktale. Have each group tape-record its tale and preserve it in a special location. Several months later, ask group members to recall the specifics of their folktale, then play the recording of their original story. Discuss the changes that occurred between the two tellings. Let students know that these changes are a normal and natural part of storytelling and give folktales their special flavor and design.

3. In a class discussion have students determine where important events took place. Have them record these events on a timeline to reinforce the sequential development of the story line. Here's an example of a simple timeline:

/_____/_____/_____/_____/_____/_____/___

Maiden   Frog   Salamander   Forest   Fish   Troll   Marriage

4. Have students locate repetitious lines throughout the book. Examples include "Many weary miles" and "Do you know of a kingdom east of the sun and west of the moon?"

5. Read *The Frog Prince* by Jane White Canfield (New York: Harper, 1970). As a class discussion, have students list similarities and differences between the two stories. This can be done by using two semantic webs—one for each story. Students can list details for each story on its appropriate semantic web.

6. Have students check the library for other versions of this story. Included could be "East of the Sun and West of the Moon" in *Norwegian Folk Tales* by P. C. Asbjørnsen and Jørgon E. Moe (New York: Viking, 1960); *East of the Sun and West of the Moon* by Kathleen Hague and Michael Hague (San Diego, CA: Harcourt Brace Jovanovich, 1980); or *East of the Sun and West of the Moon: A Play* by Nancy Willard (San Diego, CA: Harcourt Brace Jovanovich, 1989). Each version contains similarities and differences that students may wish to compare.

Science/Health

1. Students may wish to grow their own frogs. Kits are available from Holcombs Educational Materials (3205 Harvard Ave., Cleveland, OH 44105, [1-800-321-2543]). Kit 998-0125H is priced at $14.95 (at this writing) and includes a container, food, instructions, and a coupon for live tadpoles. You may also wish to check your local teacher supply store for similar kits.

2. Show the video *Tadpoles and Frogs* (National Geographic Society, Washington, DC, catalog no. 51218) to your class. Discuss the growth and development of frogs from tadpoles to adults.

3. Have students make a list of all the real animals in the book and another list of all the fictitious animals. Have them examine the list of fictitious animals to determine the real animals that closely resemble them. For example, the gila monster and Komodo dragon would be the real-life equivalents of the giant salamander. This information can be charted and shared with the class in the form of an oral report, pictures, or a display.

4. Provide students with a copy of the Beaufort wind speed chart (most science texts have one). Make arrangements to call a local weather station or the meteorologist at a local college on a daily basis to determine the average wind speed for the day. Have students record these speeds on a specially designed monthly calendar.

Art

1. Students may wish to build their own version of a troll palace. Have students bring in recycled materials such as milk cartons, cereal boxes, tin cans, and bottles, as well as loads of imagination. Glue, paint, string, and other art materials can be provided along with a scheduled period of time for completion of the project.

2. Students can create trolls from homemade clay. Here's a recipe: Mix 1 cup flour and ½ cup salt. Add ⅓ cup water, a little at a time. Squeeze the dough until it is smooth. Form into shapes; let air dry or bake at 225 degrees for 30 minutes. Paint with tempera paints. (NOTE: Adjust the recipe according to the number of students participating.)

3. Have students make their own wind socks. Form strips of construction paper into cylinders and attach colored streamers of tissue paper to the sides of the cylinders. Punch two holes in the cylinder, one on top and one on the bottom, and insert a drinking straw (the cylinder should spin freely on the straw). Stick a pin through the straw to serve as a resting place for the cylinder. Have students go outside and hold their wind socks in the wind or poke the straws into the ground for a colorful display.

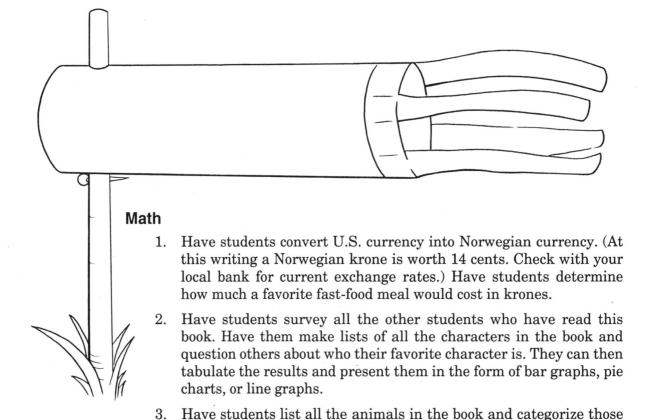

Math

1. Have students convert U.S. currency into Norwegian currency. (At this writing a Norwegian krone is worth 14 cents. Check with your local bank for current exchange rates.) Have students determine how much a favorite fast-food meal would cost in krones.

2. Have students survey all the other students who have read this book. Have them make lists of all the characters in the book and question others about who their favorite character is. They can then tabulate the results and present them in the form of bar graphs, pie charts, or line graphs.

3. Have students list all the animals in the book and categorize those animals from smallest to largest.

Music

1. Have students learn the traditional folk song "A Frog Went a Courtin' " (one version can be found in *Go in and out the Window,* arranged by Dan Fox [New York: Henry Holt, 1987]). After students learn the song they may wish to add some sound effects (frog and mouse sounds).

2. Have students create a wedding dance. They can stand in a circle, some with tambourines and recorders to provide background music. A piece of recorded classical music can also be used (e.g., Concerto for Harpsichord and Strings by Johann Sebastian Bach).

3. Students may wish to make their own recorders or flutes and invent an appropriate accompanying song for the book. Directions for making all sorts of musical instruments can be found in *Making Musical Things* by Ann Wiseman (New York: Charles Scribner's Sons, 1979).

Social Studies

1. In group discussions, have students list real places that resemble the fictitious places in the story. For example, Mountain of Ice could be the Antarctic, Father Forest could be Olympic National Forest, Great Fish of the Sea could be whales or manatees. Have students form small groups and select one area to research. They can set up a display for each area that includes maps, drawings, photographs, pictures, stories, and facts.

2. To further appreciate *Father Forest,* students may wish to contact the following organizations for materials and information regarding forests and forest conservation: National Arbor Day Foundation (100 Arbor Ave., Nebraska City, NE 68410); National Wildlife Federation (1400 16th St. NW, Washington, DC 20036); Save America's Forests (4 Library Court SE, Washington, DC 20003); Native Forest Action Council (P.O. Box 2176, Eugene, OR 97402); or Lighthawk (P.O. Box 8163, Santa Fe, NM 87504). Information gathered from these organizations can be used as a bulletin board display or a classroom learning center.

3. Some students may be interested in researching the Vikings and their explorations. They can present the information gathered from their research to the class in the form of an oral report.

Physical Education

1. Students may enjoy engaging in an obstacle course relay race replicating the maiden's travels. For example: Ice—carry ice cubes on spoons; swim—wiggle on mat to designated area; wind—blow a balloon along the floor; troll—bean bag toss at a picture of a troll.

2. Have students play a game of leapfrog over a designated course laid out on the playground.

The Great Kapok Tree
Lynne Cherry
New York: Gulliver Books, 1990

Summary

A young man enters the rain forest to cut down a Kapok tree, but the heat makes him tired and weak. The man sits down to rest and falls asleep. While he sleeps, the animals of the forest whisper in his ear not to cut down the Kapok tree. Each animal has a different reason for preserving the tree.

Critical Thinking Questions

1. If you could be one of the animals in the story, which one would you be? Why?

2. What do you think would happen if all the rain forests were eliminated?

3. What can kids do to protect the rain forests?

4. How do trees affect your life?

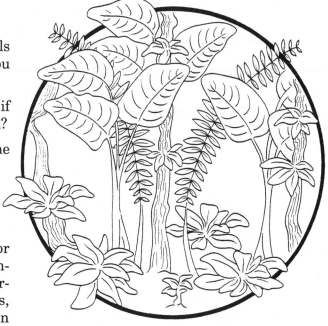

Reading/Language Arts

1. Invite students to write to one or more of the following environmental groups and ask for information, newsletters, brochures, and facts about the world's rain forests and the efforts to protect those valuable areas: Children's Rainforest (P.O. Box 936, Lewiston, ME 04240); Rainforest Action Network (450 Sansome St., Ste. 700, San Francisco, CA 94111); and Save the Rainforest (604 Jamie St., Dodgeville, WI 53533).

2. Invite students to rewrite the end of the story and tell what would have happened if the man *had* cut down the tree. This can be done in the form of letters written by the animals that used to live in the tree. Students can tell what happens to the animals now that their home is gone.

3. Get permission to plant a tree on the school grounds. Take a field trip to a local nursery to learn about the types of trees available for your area. Invite students to help with the planting and care of the tree. Students may wish to keep a class journal, writing about the planting, care, and growth of the tree and how the tree changes through the seasons. They may also want to develop a tree "baby book"—taking pictures of its first year of growth and describing its first spring, its first leaf, the first picnic under the tree, and so on.

Science/Health

1. Compare heights of the Kapok trees in the rain forest with the heights of trees commonly found in your community. Encourage students to create a chart or graph listing any significant differences.

2. Visit a local paper recycling center. Be sure to explain to students that if people recycle, millions of trees can be saved (students may be interested in learning that 60,000 trees are needed for just one run of the Sunday *New York Times*). Students may wish to create a recycling program for their families.

3. Encourage students to plant terrariums, using an old mayonnaise jar or other wide-mouth jar, to observe a mini–rain forest environment. Place a layer of clean gravel on the bottom of the jar, followed by a layer of charcoal and a layer of potting soil. Invite students to bring in small cuttings to plant in their terrariums (try to collect slow-growing plants and mosses). Students may also wish to create some tools for their terrariums such as tweezers, chopsticks, cotton swabs, long-handled spoons, and a meat baster.

Art

1. Invite students to imagine they are one of the creatures in the story. Encourage them to create a poster that says "Save Our Home." They can include a full-color drawing of the selected creature and write a convincing ad for saving the Kapok tree.

2. Invite students to create a collage of all the animals mentioned in the story. They can cut pictures and photographs from old magazines and glue them to a sheet of poster board or construction paper. Provide an opportunity for students to share the collage with others.

3. Create a rain forest environment in the classroom. Cover the walls with paper and let students paint the scenes of the rain forest, using vibrant colors. They can paint individual animals directly on the paper or create them out of papier mâché or cardboard and suspend them from the ceiling with strings. Make some of the trees and plants in relief by constructing them out of cardboard and attaching them so they stand out from the wall.

Math

1. Bring in a cross section of a tree trunk. Show students how to count rings in order to tell the age of the tree. Let students count the rings to come up with an approximate date for the tree's "birthday." Students can then write a biography of the tree, describing its contributions to the world during its lifetime.

Music

1. Several companies produce audiotapes that contain sounds of the rain forest blended with orchestral background music. Obtain one or more of these audiotapes and invite students to listen for various rain forest animals. Here are two excellent companies: NorthSound (P.O. Box 1360, Minocqua, WI 54548 [1-800-336-5666]) and The Nature Company (P.O. Box 188, Florence, KY 41022 [1-800-227-1114]).

Social Studies

1. Provide students with blank maps and invite them to color or shade in the areas of the world that have rain forests.

2. Kapok fiber is buoyant, like cork, and is often used in making life jackets. Obtain names of companies that make life jackets (the information may be obtained from your local public library or from the local Coast Guard auxiliary). Have students write to these companies asking for information on how life jackets are manufactured.

3. Invite students to create a large map of Brazil on a bulletin board or on a sheet of newsprint that has been taped to the wall. Encourage them to color in the areas of Brazil that are rain forests. Invite each student to select one of the animals illustrated on the inside jacket of the book, draw and color it with colored pencils, and attach it to the rain forest area of the map.

4. The whole class may wish to adopt an animal. Contact the American Association of Zoological Parks and Aquariums (4550 Montgomery Ave., Ste. 940N, Bethesda, MD 20814). Allow the class to decide on the type of animal to adopt and draw pictures of the adoptee to display in the room.

5. Create an ecology club. Interested students can initiate school and community projects aimed at improving the environment (see *50 Things Kids Can Do to Save the Earth*, Earthworks Group: Andrews and McMeel, 1990, for ideas). Invite local senior citizens to join the club and help out with the projects.

Physical Education

1. Invite each student to assume the role of one of the creatures in the story. Encourage each student to simulate the movements of that creature (prior library research may be necessary). Plan time to talk about the movements that are unique to each animal and how those movements help an animal survive in its environment.

Mufaro's Beautiful Daughters
John Steptoe
New York: Lothrop, Lee & Shepard, 1987

Summary

Mufaro lived in a small village in Africa with his two beautiful daughters, Nyasha and Manyara. Nyasha was kind and considerate; Manyara was selfish and spoiled. When the king announced he was looking for the most beautiful daughter in the land to be his wife, Manyara was determined to reach the city before her sister. The ending is a lesson for us all: Kindness prevails over greed.

Critical Thinking Questions

1. Do you know any other stories that are similar in plot and theme? What are they and how are they like this story?

2. How was Manyara deceptive? Do you think Mufaro would have approved of her behavior? Why?

3. Why wasn't Nyasha afraid of the snake, Nyoka, the first time she saw him?

4. Which daughter would you like to have for a friend?

5. How did the illustrations add to the story?

6. What do you think the king meant when he said that Nyasha was "the most worthy and most beautiful daughter in the land"?

7. In what ways is the daily life in the village in this story different from yours? In what ways is it alike?

Reading/Language Arts

1. Read the introductory page of the story to the students, explaining the meanings of the names of the characters in the story. Encourage students to use a name dictionary and look up the meanings of *their* names. Invite them to write their names on small pieces of poster board, decorate each with illustrations of things they enjoy doing, and write the meanings of their names underneath. These can be hung throughout the classroom.

2. Read the book *Why Mosquitoes Buzz in People's Ears* by Verna Aardema (New York: Dial Press, 1975). Explain to students that this book, like *Mufaro's Beautiful Daughters,* is an African folktale. Invite students to compare the two stories and work with a partner to generate a list of similarities and differences between them.

3. Encourage students to write a sequel to the story entitled "How Manyara Learned Kindness."

4. Read the poem "The Lion" by Jack Prelutsky (in *Random House Book of Poetry for Children* [New York: Random House, 1983]). Invite each student to choose one of the animals native to Africa and write a poem about it. Encourage students to draw their animals on construction paper and attach their poem to the body of the animal.

Science/Health

1. Plant sunflower seeds in empty margarine tubs. Keep the lids on until the seeds have sprouted. Remove the lids and place the tubs in a sunny window. Invite students to generate a list of all the products made from sunflowers. If possible, plant the seedlings on the school grounds. Students can tend the plants until they are ready to be harvested.

2. Students may be interested in setting up a "rain forest terrarium." A terrarium is a miniature controlled environment containing plants and animals.

Materials

a glass container (an old aquarium purchased at a pet store or garage sale, a large pickle jar, or even a two-liter soda bottle.)
bits of charcoal (wood charcoal from a fire or aquarium charcoal from a local pet store work equally well)

small pebbles or rocks   plants, rocks, pieces of wood
soil or potting soil   small land animals

Procedure

Be sure the container is thoroughly cleansed (and there is no soap or detergent residue left behind). Invite students to sprinkle the bottom of the container with a layer of small pebbles mixed with bits of charcoal. Follow with a layer of soil about twice as deep as the pebble-charcoal mixture. Soil from outside or potting soil (obtained from any garden center) will suffice. Invite students to sprinkle the ground with just enough water to make it moist (too much will stimulate the growth of molds). Place several plants such as mosses, ferns, lichens, small tree seedlings, and liverworts in the soil. Grass seed may be sprinkled in one section of the terrarium. Invite students to place several large rocks and decaying pieces of wood or tree branches in the terrarium, too. Students may wish to introduce small land animals such as snails, earthworms, turtles, frogs, or salamanders to the terrarium. Be sure there is sufficient food and water for the animals living there. Students should place a loosely fitting sheet of glass over the top of the terrarium (to permit the humidity level to build up). Make sure that some air can enter the terrarium, and be certain it is kept out of direct sunlight.

The terrarium will become a self-sufficient environment (check the moisture levels frequently). The plants will provide some nourishment for the animals, and the animals will provide some nourishment for the plants (it is advisable to supplement the animals' diet with food from your pet store). This terrarium is similar in many ways to life in the African rain forest, where animals and plants live in harmony with each other.

3. Students may wish to grow some rain forest plants right in the classroom. Visit a large supermarket, garden shop, or nursery and look for one or more of the following rain forest plants:

African violet	fiddle-leaf fig
begonia	orchid
bird's-nest fern	philodendron
bromeliad	prayer plant
Christmas cactus	rubber plant
corn plant	snake plant
croton	umbrella tree
dumb cane	zebra plant

Inform students that the plants they grow in the classroom will be somewhat smaller than the plants normally found throughout the African rain forest.

Art

1. Invite students to create puppets of the story characters by decorating old socks with markers, colored paper, bits of yarn, or other scraps. Divide the class into small groups and assign one scene from the story to each group. Encourage each group to paint a background for its scene on butcher paper or an old bed sheet. Hang the background on a bulletin board or use a table turned on its side for the puppet theater. For puppet ideas, consult *Children's Crafts* (a Sunset Book [San Francisco: Lane, 1976]).

2. Provide students with old white bed sheets and fabric scraps. Using the book as a guide, invite students to create costumes like the ones worn by the characters in the story. Students may wish to dramatize their favorite parts of the story.

Math

1. Invite students to work in groups to construct models of one of the houses found in Africa: Thatched roof hut, apartment house, house on stilts, adobe house, or nomadic tent. Refer to *In Africa* (by Marc Bernheim and Evelyne Bernheim [New York: Atheneum, 1975]) for ideas. Encourage them to record all the measurements and calculations necessary to construct the houses.

Music

1. Listen to the recording *Musical Instruments 3: Drums, The Music of Africa Series* by Hugh Tracey (Washington, DC: Traditional Music Documentation Project, 1972). Discuss the different rhythms produced and the types of drums used. Invite students to construct African drums by stretching pieces of vinyl or rubber across the tops of empty coffee cans that have both ends removed. Lace the edges of the vinyl together with shoestrings or other string. Encourage students to develop a code and send messages back and forth to each other.

2. Read the poem "African Dance" (by Langston Hughes) aloud to the class. Read it again and invite students to keep a steady beat with the rhythm of the poem by beating homemade drums, clapping hands, or using other rhythm instruments.

3. Use the book *The Dance of Africa: An Introduction* by Harris Petie (New York: Prentice-Hall, 1972) to teach students a traditional African dance. *The Dance, Art and Ritual of Africa* by Michael Huet (New York: Pantheon Books, 1978) provides pictures to refer to if students wish to construct dance costumes.

4. Give students an opportunity to sing in an African language by using *Call and Response Rhythmic Group Singing*, a recording by Ella Jenkins (New York: Folkways Records, 1957). This record is designed so that students repeat the words in rhythm and thus experience the language and music of Africa firsthand.

Social Studies

1. Invite students to study several maps of Africa and create an outline of the continent on the classroom floor using colored tape. Encourage students to stand around the edges of the outline, holding hands if necessary, to "become" the shape of Africa. Have students sit down in place and sing "Kumbaya"—a traditional African folk song (in *Book of Kidsongs* by Nancy Cassidy and John Cassidy [Palo Alto, CA: Klutz Press, 1986]).

2. Invite students to an African foods celebration. Bring in a variety of foods native to Africa: Honey, dates, coffee, cloves (try clove gum), yams, sunflower seeds, peanuts, grapes, and olives. Invite students to each write a paragraph describing their reactions to the foods. Encourage them to pick their favorite food.

3. Hang a large world map on one wall of the room. Invite each student to plot a travel route to Africa by making a cardboard ship and marking his or her trip (on the map) with yarn. Attach the ships so that they can travel freely along the string from the United States to Africa. Students may wish to write a story describing their feelings as they begin their trip to Africa, including what they expect to see or do along the way.

Physical Education

1. Invite students to map out and construct a walking path around the school grounds. They can use this path as part of regular physical fitness activities or as part of a nature trail through selected areas of plant life near the school. You may wish to talk about the benefits of walking as a lifelong physical activity for everybody.

Sky Tree
Thomas Locker
New York: HarperCollins, 1995

Summary

A tree stands on a hill by a river. The sky changes, the seasons change, and the tree goes through a series of marvelous transformations. Wonderful paintings highlight significant events in the year of a single tree.

Critical Thinking Questions

1. Which of the illustrations made you feel the happiest, the saddest, the quietest, or the smallest?

2. Why do you think this tree is called the Sky Tree?

3. How is this tree similar to or different from other trees you know?

Reading/Language Arts

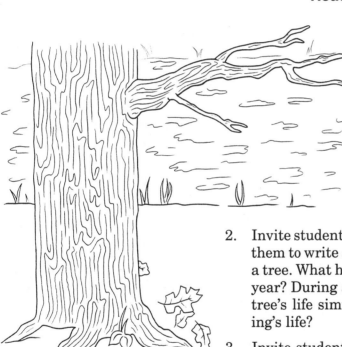

1. Invite students to write to one or more of the following groups and ask for information on trees: Forest Service, U.S. Department of Agriculture, P.O. Box 96090, Washington, DC 20090 (ask for the poster "How a Tree Grows"); National Arbor Day Foundation, 100 Arbor Ave., Nebraska City, NE 68410 (ask for information on Arbor Day).

2. Invite students to imagine they are trees. Encourage them to write a life story told from the perspective of a tree. What happens to a tree during the course of a year? During a decade? During a century? How is a tree's life similar to or different from a human being's life?

3. Invite students to write to the National Arbor Day Foundation (100 Arbor Ave., Nebraska City, NE 68410) and request a copy of *The Conservation Trees* brochure. This brochure explains how trees help the environment. Invite students to draft a similar document that would apply to the trees in your particular area of the country.

4. Invite an employee of a local garden center or nursery to visit the classroom and discuss the types of trees that are native to your area of the country. What are some planting techniques? How should trees be cared for? Why are some trees easier to grow than others? Invite students to gather the responses to those questions

as well as their own into an informative brochure or leaflet that could be distributed at the garden center or nursery.

5. Here are some great tree books you may wish to share with your students: *Tree* by David Burnie (New York: Knopf, 1988); *Green Giants* by Sneed Collard (Minocqua, WI: NorthWord Press, 1994); *Mighty Tree* by Dick Gackenbach (San Diego, CA: Harcourt Brace, 1992); *Trees* by Linda Gamlin (New York: Dorling Kindersley, 1993); *Forests* by David Lambert (Mahwah, NJ: Troll, 1990); *Song for the Ancient Forest* by Nancy Luenn (New York: Atheneum, 1993); *Outside and Inside Trees* by Sandra Markle (New York: Bradbury, 1993); and *The Tree in the Ancient Forest* by Carol Reed-Jones (Nevada City, CA: Dawn Publications, 1995).

6. Plan time to discuss some of the questions presented throughout the book. Which ones are subject to the widest interpretations?

Science/Health

1. Invite students to select a tree near the school. Encourage them to take periodic photographs of the tree throughout the year and maintain a diary or journal of the changes in the tree. Who comes to visit the tree (animals)? Does the tree change colors? What does the tree look like when it rains, snows, or is sunny outside? Periodically, talk with students about any changes in the tree and how those changes may be similar to or different from those experienced by the Sky Tree.

2. Trees for Life (1103 Jefferson, Wichita, KS 67203) is an organization that uses its profits to plant fruit trees in underdeveloped countries. For a fee of 50 cents per student, the organization will send you seeds, individual cartons for planting, and a teacher notebook. The type of tree it sends will depend on the state in which you live; it sends only trees that are native to your region. Students will enjoy watching their seeds sprout and finally grow into trees.

Art

1. Invite students to use a Polaroid camera to take photographs of a single object (e.g., a tree) throughout the course of the day. They can then place their photos side by side to note any differences or subtle changes in the photos (i.e., length of shadow, change in coloration, visiting animals, etc.). Plan time for students to discuss those changes and the effect on their interpretation of the object.

2. Invite students to each select an identical outdoor object and draw it using colored pencils. Plan time afterward to discuss any similarities or differences in the drawings. What led each student to interpret the object in the way he or she did?

3. Invite students to give some thought to the colors associated with each of the seasons. For example, what colors would they associate with winter? White (the color of snow) would be a logical selection, but they should also consider white plants, white animals, and white objects. What other colors besides white could be used to describe winter? What colors describe summer?—perhaps orange, the color of the blazing sun; green, the color of deep forest trails; and yellow, the color of birds flitting in and out of trees. Invite students to make charts or graphs of the colors associated with each of the seasons and the plants and animals that display those colors.

Math

1. Discuss the importance of recycling newspapers to save trees. Explain that approximately every 4-foot stack of newspapers equals the wood from one tree. Designate one corner of your room or hallway as a newspaper recycling center. Invite students to begin saving newspapers and stacking them in the designated area. Once a week, measure the stack of newspapers and record the measurement on a chart, placing a figure of a tree on the chart each time 4 feet of newspapers is collected.

2. Invite students to locate a tall tree they wish to measure. Select one student and invite someone to measure that student's height with a yardstick. Take a strip of white paper (about 1 x 4 inches) and pin it to the tree at that student's height. Invite the student to walk away from the tree, holding the yardstick vertically at arm's length, until the strip is level with the 1-inch mark on the yardstick. Invite the student to note where the treetop reaches on the inch scale on the yardstick. Invite the student to multiply that mark by his or her height. The result will be the exact height of the tree (see figure below).

Example: The student's height is 54 inches. Distance sighted on the yardstick from base of tree to top is 7 inches.

54 x 7= 378 inches (or 31.5 feet). The tree is 31.5 feet tall.

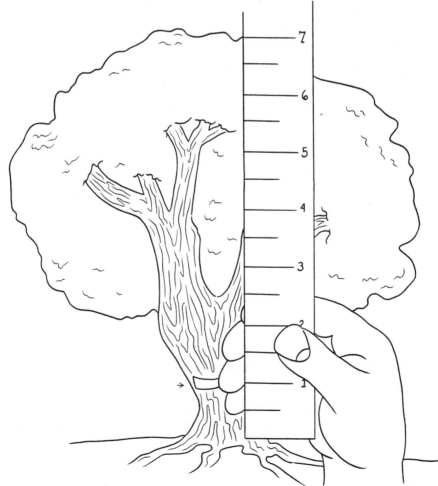

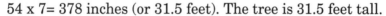

Music

1. Invite students to interview the school's music teacher as well as any local musicians on those instruments that are made entirely or partially from wood. How many of the instruments in an orchestra are woodwinds? If all the instruments that had wood in them were eliminated from an orchestra, what instruments would remain?

Social Studies

1. Invite youngsters to select books from the school or public library in which legends are used to explain seasons, weather conditions, stars and constellations, or forces of nature. Native American legends (*Star Tales: North American Indian Stories About the Stars* by G. Mayo [New York: Walker, 1987]) and Asian tales (*A Song of Stars: An Asian Legend* by T. Birdeye [New York: Holiday, 1990]) offer excellent examples of legends, myths, and stories handed down through the generations to explain the unexplainable. Invite children to gather a collection of books about the seasons written in a "legendary" format. What similarities do they notice? What differences? Why are legends created in the first place? Why do these legends seem to stay around for long periods of time?

   After youngsters have had an opportunity to share various legends from different cultures, invite them to create their own legend about the seasons. They should include some factual data to give the story a sense of authenticity as well as some creative and interpretive explanations of events. Provide opportunities for children to share these stories with others.

Physical Education

1. Invite a local expert to your class to explain orienteering (contact a local hiking club or scouting group). Invite the visitor to take the class through a demonstration of orienteering on the school grounds or in any nearby woods.

Surprising Swimmers
Anthony D. Fredericks
Minnetonka, MN: NorthWord Press, 1996

Summary

This book provides young scientists with an amazing and fascinating look at some of nature's most unusual creatures. There's a bird that "flies" underwater, an insect that swims backward and upside down, snakes that stay underwater for more than three hours, and an animal that spends its whole life on a bubble raft. Colorful illustrations and incredible photographs highlight this engrossing book.

Critical Thinking Questions

1. Which of the 12 animals in this book did you find most interesting? What did you learn about those animals?

2. Do any of the animals in this book swim in ways that humans do? Would you classify humans as "surprising swimmers"?

3. What other forms of travel or transportation do animals use?

4. What other animals do you think should have been included in this book?

Reading/Language Arts

1. There are many phrases and sayings in which animals and water are matched. These include "it's raining cats and dogs," "swims like a fish," and "dog paddle." Invite students to collect other terms, phrases, or sayings in which an animal or animals are matched with water.

---

2. Encourage students to write to the following organizations and request any brochures or information they have available on marine conservation: The Center for Marine Conservation (1725 DeSales St. NW, Washington, DC 20036) and National Wildlife Federation (1400 16th St. NW, Washington, DC 20036).

Science/Health

1. Talk with students about some of the "fantastic facts" included throughout this book. Which ones did they find to be most amazing? Why? Why did the author include those facts?

2. Students may wish to observe their own "classroom swimmers" in action. Here's an activity that will help them do just that:

Materials

brine shrimp eggs (available from any pet store)
noniodized kosher salt (available at most grocery stores)
two-quart pot   medicine dropper
water   hand lens or inexpensive microscope
teaspoon   aged tap water

Procedure

Fill the pot with 2 quarts of water and allow it to sit for two days, stirring it occasionally. (Most city water has chlorine, which would kill the shrimp. "Aging" it for several days allows the chlorine gas to escape from the water.) Mix 5 teaspoons of noniodized salt with the water until dissolved. Add ½ teaspoon brine shrimp eggs to the salt water and place the pot in a warm spot. Invite students to use the medicine dropper to remove some eggs from the water and observe them with a hand lens or microscope. They may wish to check a drop of water every day. They also may wish to create a series of drawings or illustrations that record the growth of the brine shrimp.

The brine shrimp eggs will begin to hatch in about two days. They will continue to grow in the water until they reach their adult stage. Students will be able to watch this growth process over a period of many days.

NOTE: Brine shrimp eggs that are purchased at a pet store are the fertilized eggs of very tiny animals—called brine shrimp. The eggs are dried and can be kept for very long periods (especially when kept in a dry place). When they are added to the salt water, the eggs "wake up" and begin to grow. Although the shrimp are very small, students can watch them grow for many days. Brine shrimp eggs are sold as fish food for aquariums. Make sure students do not try to eat them.

3. Here's a simple activity that will demonstrate how a baleen whale obtains krill (one of the creatures in this book).

Materials

a sink filled with cold water
a packet of dry vegetable soup
a kitchen strainer

Procedure

Invite students to fill a kitchen sink with cold, clear water and to open and sprinkle the packet of vegetable soup over the surface of the water (they'll note that the soup does not sink but rather floats on the surface). Have them hold the kitchen strainer in one hand and skim it slowly over the surface of the water. Point out that the vegetable pieces are caught in the strainer and the water passes through the wire mesh. When students lift the strainer out of the water, it contains a wide variety of "food."

Baleen whales sift their food in much the same way students did with the strainer. However, their food isn't floating on the surface but rather swims through the water. The baleen combs allow a whale to swim through its dinner, strain the water from the plant or animal life, and eat what remains on its baleen. As students might imagine, this is a very efficient form of eating as long as there is sufficient food in the water. For example, one blue whale needs to eat about 4 tons of krill every *day* in order to survive. That's a lot of food to strain from the water!

Art

1. Invite students to create posters or advertisements to attract other students to this book. What information, data, or illustrations should be included? Students may wish to hang their posters or advertisements in the school library.

2. Invite a local artist to visit your classroom and describe some of the procedures used in illustrating a book or advertisement. How does the artist take advantage of color, "white space," size, dimension, and perspective in deciding how a final illustration will look? Invite the artist to describe some of the artistic techniques used in the book's illustrations.

Math

1. Just like trees, fish have rings on their scales. Students can use these rings to determine the age of a fish. Here's how:

Materials

a fish
dark construction paper
hand lens or magnifying glass

Procedure

Invite students to remove four or five scales from the fish. (You may want to assist them.) Pliers work to gently pull off selected scales. Place the scales on the dark construction paper and use the hand lens to examine each one.

As fish grow they develop bands, or rings, on their scales. As students look at a fish scale they'll probably notice (depending on the species) that a scale has both wide bands and thin bands. The wide bands represent growth in summer, when there is a lot of food for the fish to eat. The thin bands represent growth during the winter months. Also, students might notice that the wide bands are lighter in color than the thin bands. Because fish grow more slowly during the winter months, the bands are darker.

Since a year is made up of both summer and winter months, a full year's growth (for a fish) is represented by one wide band plus one thin band (or one dark band plus one light band). In order to determine how old the fish was, students can simply count the total number of wide bands, or rings, on a scale. Invite students to assemble several fish and calculate and chart the age(s) of those fish.

Music

1. If possible, obtain ocean- or water-related music to share with students. An excellent source of "environmental music" is *NorthSound* (P.O. Box 1360, Minocqua, WI 54548 [1-800-336-6398]). You may wish to play some of this music while students are working on various activities or invite students to listen to a selected tape and identify all the "surprising swimmers" they can.

Social Studies

1. Provide students with a desk or wall map of the world. Invite them to place a short piece of masking tape (with the name of an animal written on it) at each of the countries mentioned in the book. Students may wish to visit the public or school library and read about other types of animals that inhabit those countries.

Physical Education

1. Invite students to contact the swimming coach at the local high school or a certified swimming instructor at a community pool. Invite that individual to visit the classroom and demonstrate weight-lifting and body-building activities that are particularly suited for competitive swimmers. Invite students to collect that information and present it in the form of a brochure or leaflet.

The True Story of the 3 Little Pigs
Jon Scieszka
New York: Penguin Books, 1989

Summary

A riotous retelling of the classic tale about the big bad wolf and the three little pigs—except this time the wolf gets to tell his side of the story. The wolf acts as his own reporter just to make sure the facts are correct, and the result is an uproariously funny story that kids will want to read over and over again.

Critical Thinking Questions

1. What do you think was the funniest part of this story? Please explain.

2. How does this story differ from the original version of the story?

3. If you could write a letter to the author, what would you like to say?

4. If you could give the story a different ending, what would you write?

Reading/Language Arts

1. Invite students to select one or more familiar stories (e.g., "The Three Billy Goats Gruff," "Little Red Riding Hood," "Cinderella," or "Hansel and Gretel"). Encourage them to retell or rewrite a version of the selected story from the point of view of a different character. For example, "Cinderella" could be told from the point of view of one of the three stepsisters, "Little Red Riding Hood" could be retold from the grandmother's point of view, or "Jack and the Beanstalk" could be rewritten from the giant's point of view. Plan time for students to share their retellings with other members of the class.

2. Invite students to select a familiar nursery rhyme or fairy tale and write it as a newspaper article. In other words, how would a newspaper reporter write a story about a little girl (in a red riding hood) traveling through the forest on her way to her grandmother's house? How would a reporter handle a story about a woman who works for seven little men (Snow White)?

3. Involve students in a readers theatre adaptation of the original "Three Little Pigs." Readers theatre is an oral interpretation of a piece of literature read in a dramatic style. Students use prepared scripts (no memorization is necessary) to present an adaptation of a familiar tale. The following readers theatre script (from *Frantic Frogs and Other Frankly Fractured Folktales for Readers Theatre* by Anthony D. Fredericks [Englewood, CO: Teacher Ideas Press, 1993]) is a (slightly wacky) presentation of this story.

THE REALLY REALLY <u>REALLY</u> TRUE STORY OF THE THREE LITTLE PIGS

STAGING: The narrator is at a lectern or podium near the front of the staging area. The three pigs are on stools or chairs. The wolf is standing and moves back and forth between the other characters.

Very Smart Pig	Average Pig	Not Too Bright Pig
X	X	X

	Mean and Grouchy Wolf	
	X	

Narrator		
X		

NARRATOR: A long time ago, when fairy tales used to be inhabited by animals who could talk and think, there lived these three pigs. Ya, ya, ya, I know what you're saying—each of them built a house and along comes this mean old wolf with incredibly bad breath who blows down the first two houses because they weren't built according to the local zoning laws and then tries to blow down the third house—which is, incidentally, made of reinforced concrete, not bricks—and he eventually falls into a big pot of boiling water and the three pigs live happily ever after, at least until their mother finds out what they've been doing and sends them to bed without their dinner. Well, that's probably the story you heard when you were a tiny tyke—but, that's not the really real story. Actually, your parents couldn't tell you the really real story 'cause it was filled with all kinds of violence and a couple of bad words. Well, now that you're all grown up and very mature, we're going to tell you the really really *really* true story of the three little pigs—but, of course, we're going to have to leave out all those bad words.

So, anyway there was this big old farm and on the farm lived these three brothers who, as you know by now, were pigs. And, as you also know, they were talking pigs. So, one day they were sitting in the living room of their mother's four bedroom condominium going over some of the latest issues of *Better Homes and Gardens*. And that's where the really really *really* true story of the three little pigs begins.

VERY SMART PIG: Hey, brothers, you know it's about time we moved on out of Mom's house. We're grown up now and ready to go out into the world to seek our fortune. And besides, Mom's getting on in years and won't be able to support us much longer. In fact, pretty soon we're going to have to think about putting her in the Old Porker's Home.

AVERAGE PIG: You know, brother, you've got a point there. Besides we wouldn't have much of a story if all we did was sit around Mom's living room discussing the color of her drapes or "500 Uses for Bacon Bits."

NOT TOO BRIGHT PIG: Ya! It sure is getting crowded in here, too. You know, since we're pigs we don't clean up after ourselves, we track mud all over the place, and we make funny grunting noises for most of the day. I think the neighbors are beginning to wonder what we really do. We better move out while we still can.

NARRATOR: And so it was that the three brothers decided to move out of Mom's house and buy some property out in the country. The real estate agent assured them that the land was ideal—rolling hills, lots of space, and no strange or weird animals in the nearby forest.

MEAN AND GROUCHY WOLF: (insulted) Hey, wait a minute! Aren't I supposed to have a place in this story, too?

NARRATOR: (forcefully) Hey, keep your shirt on! We'll sneak you over from the Red Riding Hood story and no one will be the wiser. In fact, if you play your cards right, you can finish this story and get back to grandma's house in time to hop back into her pajamas and wait for that stupid Riding Hood girl to come along.

MEAN AND GROUCHY WOLF: O.K., O.K. But just make it quick, buster. You know what the wolf's union says about me doing double time?

NARRATOR: Anyway, as I was saying, the three pigs began to build their dream houses along the country road that ran through their property.

From *The Integrated Curriculum, Second Edition.* © 1998 Anthony D. Fredericks. Teacher Ideas Press. (800) 237-6124.

NOT TOO
BRIGHT PIG: You know, I'm not very smart, so I think I'll build my house out of straw. So, who cares if it blows down in the first windstorm of the season or leaks like a sieve in the winter.

MEAN AND GROUCHY
WOLF: (insulted) Hey, now hold on a minute here! Do you honestly think I would want to waste my time with this stupid little porker here. You know, I've got far better things to do with my time than wait until this little idiot builds his stupid little house of straw for me to come prancing down this lane to huff and puff and blow it down. That's got to be an absolute waste of my finely tuned acting talents!

NARRATOR: Well then, what if we move this story along and see what Average Pig does.

MEAN AND GROUCHY
WOLF: Well, O.K., but this better be a lot more interesting than that stupid little hambone with the pile of hay in his back yard.

NARRATOR: Hey, just settle down! Don't have a coronary! Just let me see what I can do with this part of the story. It's all yours, Average Pig.

AVERAGE
PIG: Thanks. While you guys were talking I was just walking around my property gathering some sticks and branches and tree limbs. I think that I'll build my house out of this stuff. It may not be too sturdy, but at least it won't fall down the first time I slam the front door. Of course, the local fire marshal may have a thing or two to say about it.

MEAN AND GROUCHY
WOLF: (angrily) Now just a gosh darn minute here! You want me to believe that this walking pile of pork chops is really going to build a house of sticks so that I can come along and blow it down just like I was supposed to do with his brother's house. Come on, get real! I mean, what a waste! Why would I even want to take the time to huff and puff my way around this stupid little structure? You know, you guys are really starting to tick me off. All I can say is, this story better get a lot better and real fast, too!

NARRATOR: Boy, you sure do get pushy. You know, this is supposed to be a story about the three little pigs, not about some wolf with an attitude problem.

MEAN AND GROUCHY
WOLF: Look, wise guy, how'd you like me to nibble on your face? If I want to take the lead role in this story, then I'm going to. After all, just look what my brothers and I have been putting up with in all those other stories.

NARRATOR: (indignant) Now, just hold on. We still have to see what Very Smart Pig does with his part in the story.

VERY SMART
PIG: You know, they don't call me Very Smart Pig for nothin'. In fact, I'm the guy they call on to bring home the bacon . . . get it? . . . bring home the bacon! So, while this hot shot wolf might be trying to huff and puff down some flimsy houses built by my two less than brilliant brothers, I was constructing a house completely out of bricks and steel and reinforced cement. Ain't nobody going to blow this baby down! I mean this beauty is built!!! And any wolf who has any kind of smarts would do well to just keep his distance. I mean we're talkin' *SOLID* here!

MEAN AND GROUCHY
WOLF: (very angry) Look, I'm not takin' any gruff from no lard-faced pig. I'll huff and puff my way across the whole county if I want to. I'll blow down, damage, and destroy as many houses as I want.

VERY SMART
PIG: (angry) Yea, you and whose army?

MEAN AND GROUCHY
WOLF: (angry) Hey, watch it pork breath. How would you like me to turn you into a pile of ham sandwiches?

VERY SMART
PIG: (very angry) Yea, just go ahead and try it.

MEAN AND GROUCHY
WOLF: (extremely angry) Just watch me.

NARRATOR: All day long, Very Smart Pig and Mean and Grouchy Wolf argued about who was the strongest and who was the smartest. In fact, Wolf and Pig went far into the night with their argument and for all we know they're still arguing away. But, of course, that would never make for an exciting story for the kiddies. So a long time ago a bunch of fairy tale writers got together and decided to spice up the story a bit and turn the wolf into a door-to-door salesman with an asthma problem. The rest, as they say, is history. And now, you know the really really *really* true story of the three little pigs.

SOURCE: Fredericks, Anthony D. *Frantic Frogs and Other Frankly Fractured Folktales for Readers Theatre.* Englewood, CO: Teacher Ideas Press, 1993. Used by permission.

Science/Health

1. Despite their reputation, pigs cannot overeat. They have a natural hormone (known as *cholecystokinin*) that acts as a messenger from the brain to the stomach "telling" the pig when it's time to stop eating. This appetite suppressant is being researched as an aid for human dieters. Students can begin to understand the digestive process (in humans) with the following activity: In each of three small plastic cups, pour 3 tablespoons of milk. In the first cup, put 2 tablespoons of water. Cover the cup with a sheet of plastic wrap, using a rubber band to hold the wrap in place. In the second cup, put 2 tablespoons of a weak acid such as lemon juice or vinegar and cover as before. In the third cup, put 2 tablespoons of an enzyme such as a meat tenderizer and cover as before. After one or two hours invite students to observe the changes that occur in each cup. (The changes that occur in cups 2 and 3 are similar to the digestive process in the human stomach.)

2. Pigs cannot sweat. They lie in mud not because they are sloppy but rather because mud helps keep their bodies cool. The following experiment will help students learn about their own sweat glands: Mix together ½ cup water and 2 teaspoons of corn starch. Stir well. Cut some paper toweling into several 2-x-2-inch squares and dip them in the liquid. Set them aside to dry. Work with students and paint one of their palms with iodine (this should be done only by an adult). Encourage youngsters to engage in a strenuous physical activity for a time (they should build up a sweat). Invite them to place one of the paper towel squares on their iodine-covered palm. The sweat glands on that palm will show up as dark spots. Students will also notice that sweat glands seem to be concentrated in selected areas of the skin.

Art

1. Invite students to create an oversized collage of pig pictures and illustrations cut out of several different magazines. How many different versions of pigs can they locate?

2. Invite students to create a wordless picture book using important events from the story. This activity can be done in small groups with each group displaying its book on the bulletin board. What challenges are there in creating a wordless

version of this story? What will students need to consider in order to maintain the humor in the story?

Math

1. This story begins when the wolf runs out of sugar in baking a cake for his granny's birthday. Invite students to work with you in preparing a special birthday cake for the wolf's granny. Focus on the measurements needed in order to properly prepare the cake. What adjustments would have to be made in the basic recipe in order to serve everyone in the class?

Music

1. Work with the school's music teacher to compile a collection of songs related to pigs and farm animals. Plan opportunities when students can share these songs in class.

Social Studies

1. If possible, invite a speaker from the county extension agency or farm bureau to visit your class and talk about the role of pigs in the farming community. What are some of the challenges pig farmers face? How do they deal with those challenges? Are pigs easier or harder to raise than other types of livestock?

2. If possible, obtain a copy of the National Geographic video *Animals on the Farm* (catalog no. A51498, National Geographic Society, Educational Services, Washington, DC 20036 [1-800-368-2728]). Discuss with students the importance of farms to the economy of the country and the contributions of farmers to our everyday lives.

Physical Education

1. Invite students to create a physical-fitness guide for pigs. What activities or exercises could pigs practice (on a daily basis) to maintain proper physical conditioning?

Volcanoes
Seymour Simon
New York: Morrow, 1988

Summary

In an extraordinary book, readers get to explore some of the most amazing and majestic volcanoes in the world. They learn that volcanoes, for all their fiery splendor and destruction, produce new mountains, new islands, and new soil. An unforgettable journey.

Critical Thinking Questions

1. What was the most amazing thing you learned in this book?

2. Did the author change your mind about what a volcano does?

3. What do you think would be the consequences if a volcano erupted in your local area?

4. Which of the volcanoes mentioned in the book would you like to visit? Why?

Reading/Language Arts

1. Invite youngsters to watch the filmstrip *Earthquakes and Volcanoes* (available from the National Geographic Society, Washington, DC, 20026, as part of the *Discovering the Powers of Nature* series [catalog no. 03237]). Invite them to generate a list of adjectives (to be recorded in a homemade book) to describe the actions they observed.

2. Invite students to write letters to people who have lived in the area of a volcanic eruption (e.g., the people who lived near Mt. St. Helens) and solicit information about their experiences.

3. Encourage students to investigate the myths and legends of volcanoes compared with modern scientific knowledge.

Science/Health

1. Obtain some volcanic ash. Mix different amounts with equal amounts of potting soil. Fill several compartments of a egg carton with the different mixtures and plant several vegetable seeds in each compartment. Encourage students to compare the relative growth rates of the vegetables. In which growth medium do the seeds germinate first? Which one is most conducive to healthy growth? How does the amount of volcanic ash affect the germination and growth of plants?

2. Take two paraffin blocks and cut them into the shape of earth-crust plates. Put them on foil on a hot plate (low setting) and slowly move them in opposite directions (using heavy-duty gloves) to examine how plates move and react. Wax can burn, be careful.

3. Invite students to compare the photographs in this book with volcano photos in other books. What are some similarities and differences? How can they account for the differences in photos of the same volcanoes?

4. Show one of the "before" photos in the book and invite students to make predictions on what a volcano will look like after an eruption (they may wish to draw illustrations). Afterward, compare their predictions with a succeeding photo in the book.

Art

1. Invite students to draw their own interpretations of the two gods, Vulcan and Pele. Gather the pictures in a scrapbook.

2. Invite students to create a flip book illustrating the sequence of activities during a volcanic eruption.

3. Encourage students to place the names of the four different kinds of volcanoes on separate sheets of paper. Invite them to draw illustrations of selected examples (from around the world) of each type of volcano.

4. Invite students to create a scrapbook that classifies volcanic rocks (lava, pumice, etc.) and types of lava (aa, pahoehoe).

Math

1. Invite students to make charts of the dormancy periods of selected volcanoes. For example, which volcanoes have remained dormant the longest? Which volcanoes have had the most recent eruptions? Where are the most dormant volcanoes located? Where are the most active volcanoes located?

2. Invite children to locate information on the "eruption rates" (the length of time from the start of the volcano until it "settles down") for different volcanoes. How can they account for the wide variation in rates?

3. Invite students to measure the temperatures of different things in the household (e.g., boiling water, microwave dinner) and compare those temperatures with the temperature of molten lava (they can make and post comparative charts).

4. Encourage students to investigate the heights of different active and inactive volcanoes around the world. During a volcanic eruption, how much of the mountain is lost?

5. Invite students to compare the time periods of volcanoes and earthquakes. Why do volcanoes tend to last longer? Why do active volcanoes and major earthquakes occur in the same areas of the world?

6. Encourage students to obtain data on the relative speeds of different types of lava. How fast does quick-moving lava flow in comparison with slow-moving lava?

Music

1. Invite children to develop a pantomime, song, or dance in which they simulate the actions of the volcano, lava, surrounding territory, and so on.

Social Studies

1. Invite students to construct comparative charts of volcanoes according to different climatic regions of the world (e.g., how many active volcanoes are located in tropical regions versus in polar regions?).

2. Invite children to study famous volcanoes in history (e.g., Krakatoa, Mt. Fuji, Vesuvius).

Physical Education

1. Invite students to watch a video of a volcano erupting (e.g., *The Violent Earth* [National Geographic Society, Washington, DC 20036, catalog no. 51234]). Encourage students to pretend they are actually at the site of one of the eruptions. Invite them to plan evacuation procedures. What physical activities would be necessary in order to effectively execute those procedures?

The Wednesday Surprise
Eve Bunting
New York: Clarion Books, 1989

Summary

Wednesday nights are special for Anna. That's when Grandma comes over with a big, lumpy bag filled with books. Together they read story after story, all the time planning a surprise for Dad's birthday.

Critical Thinking Questions

1. Why do you think Anna's grandmother wanted to learn to read?

2. Why was Anna's father so happy?

3. If Anna's grandmother could relive her life, what do you think she would do differently?

4. What are some of your favorite family moments?

5. What are some of your favorite birthday memories?

Reading/Language Arts

1. Encourage students to create an oath to read with their parents at least 15 minutes each day. Students may wish to design a contract to be signed by them and their parents.

2. Students may enjoy creating a family newspaper. They can be reporters and interview family members about their opinions on current issues, hobbies and free-time activities, and vacation spots, for example. The information on each family can be assembled into a sheet of news and all the sheets collected into a large family newspaper.

3. Invite a member of the local literacy council or reading council to visit your classroom and discuss illiteracy. Encourage your students to ask questions about the extent of the problem and what efforts are being mounted to overcome it.

4. Schedule a family "read-in." Invite parents, grandparents, and other adults to visit the classroom at a scheduled time (during the schoolday, immediately after school, or in the evening). Direct each person to bring a collection of favorite books and a pillow or two. Schedule a block of time (e.g., one hour) for everyone to gather in a central location and read silently. Afterward, individuals may wish to share some of their thoughts or things learned via their reading.

Science/Health

1. Do you remember baking cookies with your grandmother? I do! Here's a recipe for no-bake cookies your students may enjoy preparing on their own (or with your guidance).

✂ *No-Bake Cookies*

INGREDIENTS

2 c. granulated sugar	1 tsp. salt
½ c. water	½ c. peanut butter
½ c. cocoa	1 tsp. vanilla
4 tbsp. butter	3 c. quick oats

DIRECTIONS

Combine sugar, water, cocoa, butter, and salt in a saucepan. Boil for one minute. Add peanut butter, vanilla, and oats. Cool slightly. Drop by spoonfuls onto wax paper and allow to set.

 -

After students have prepared their cookies, invite them to discuss all the scientific principles operating throughout the preparation process (use of simple machines, creation of mixtures and compounds, effects of temperature, etc.). Students may wish to compile a booklet of all the scientific processes that took place during the creation of their cookies.

Art

1. Encourage students to create a collage (pictures and words cut from old magazines and glued to a sheet of poster board) of all the things that are important to a family (e.g., love, sharing, conversation, listening, caring).

2. Invite students to create posters on the importance of reading for all individuals—children and adults. Get permission from several local businesses to hang the posters in their store windows or near the cash registers. Periodically create new posters and rotate them every so often.

3. Provide students with modeling clay and ask each one to create a bust of a favorite family member. Discuss why a particular person was selected. After all the busts are completed, set up a gallery of busts in the classroom.

Math

1. Invite students to create special charts or graphs of literacy activities in your classroom. For example, number of books read during a selected time period (e.g., one month); number of minutes spent reading at home; number of minutes spent reading versus number of minutes spent watching TV; and number of books checked out of the school library during a marking period. Students may wish to compare their figures with those of another classroom.

2. Students may be interested in creating a family timeline. Have them ask their parents about the marriage dates, birth dates, and deaths of various family members. Invite students to record these dates on a timeline to be put up on one wall of the classroom. (Each date can be recorded on an index card. Lengths of string can be strung across one wall of the room. Clothespins can be used to clip the index cards to the string in the correct order.)

Music

1. Invite students to think of a theme song for this book. What popular tune would be appropriate as background music when reading the book to others? Invite students to defend their choices.

Social Studies

1. Invite students to gather data on the literacy rates of various countries around the world. Which countries have the highest literacy rates? Invite them to discuss why the United States does not have the highest literacy rate of all of the industrialized countries.

2. Invite students to create a large class scrapbook of the activities they enjoy doing with their grandparents. The scrapbook could include photographs with accompanying captions as well as illustrations of holidays or family gatherings.

3. Encourage students to conduct an interview with the oldest living relative in their family. The interview can be conducted in person, by telephone, or by mail. Invite students to inquire about some of the most memorable events of their relatives as well as some of the reading materials they may have used when they were children. Provide opportunities for students to share their discoveries in writing or orally.

4. All families celebrate holidays differently. Set up a bulletin board for students to post descriptions and photographs of family celebrations and special events.

5. Invite students to bring in photographs of various family members. Have them put push pins in a large world map indicating the country of origin of members of the family and post the pictures next to the countries of origin.

Physical Education

1. Invite students to put together a booklet or information sheet on selected physical-fitness activities for older adults. What types of activities are most appropriate? Can activities designed for younger people be modified for older people?

GRADE 5

Clever Camouflagers

Anthony D. Fredericks
Minnetonka, MN: NorthWord Press, 1997

Summary

In this amazing book, readers will see and learn about some of nature's masters of disguise. These include fish that look like seaweed, birds that turn white in winter, lizards that change color a dozen times a day, and even plants that look like stones. Lots of incredible information and fantastic facts highlight this colorful book.

Critical Thinking Questions

1. Which of the creatures was most amazing?

2. If you had the opportunity to camouflage yourself, what would you look like?

3. What are some other "clever camouflagers" that could have been included in this book?

4. Why is it so important for some animals to disguise themselves? What might be some disadvantages?

5. What ways do humans protect themselves from their enemies?

Reading/Language Arts

1. Invite each student to choose an animal from the book to study. Students can write a newspaper birth announcement for their animal. They will need to do some research to collect necessary information. Provide the birth announcement section of daily newspapers for students to use as a reference. Decorate a bulletin board to look like a section of a newspaper, and hang the animal birth announcements there. Students can include an illustration of the new baby.

2. Several of the animals mentioned in this book are endangered, others live in very specific environments, and a few are fascinating simply because they do things no other animals do. Children can learn more about these and other animals throughout the world by obtaining copies of or subscribing to one or more of the following children's magazines:

> *Audubon Adventure* (National Audubon Society, 613 Riversville Rd., Greenwich, CT 06830); *Chickadee* (Young Naturalists Foundation, P.O. Box 11314, Des Moines, IA 50340); *Dolphin Log* (Cousteau Society, 8430 Santa Monica Blvd., Los Angeles, CA 90069); *Naturescope* (National Wildlife Federation, 1912 16th St., NW, Washington, DC 20036); *Ranger Rick* (National Wildlife Federation, 1412 16th St., NW, Washington, DC 20036); *Zoobooks* (Wildlife Education, Ltd., 930 West Washington St., San Diego, CA 92103).

Science/Health

1. Encourage students to keep an animal journal, a record of all the animals they see during the week. They should include pets, wild animals, insects, and animals seen on television. Hang posters for mammals, fish, birds, reptiles and amphibians, and so on. Students can add to the charts daily.

2. Invite youngsters to keep a journal of the activities, habits, travels, and motions of a single animal. Kids may want to select a house pet or some other animal that can be observed quite regularly throughout the day. Provide youngsters with a field journal, a simple notebook wildlife biologists frequently use to track the activities of one or more wild animals over the course of an extended period of time.

3. Invite students to complete the following list, using animals from the book. Encourage them to research other "clever camouflagers" and add them to this list or an oversized wall chart posted in the classroom.

ANIMAL	*CAMOUFLAGE TECHNIQUE*
Chameleon	Can change its skin color to match surroundings
Walking stick	
Bittern	Resembles swaying grass
Ptarmigan	
Sargassum fish	
Orchid praying mantis	Looks like a flower part
Decorator crab	
Tree hopper	
Leaf fish	
Katydid	
Flounder	Colors match ocean bottom

4. Invite children to go outside and select a section of grassy area (part of a yard, lawn, or playground). Have them push four sharpened pencils into the soil in a 1-foot-square pattern and tie string around the pencils, making a miniature "boxing ring" on the ground. Invite them to get on their hands and knees and look closely

inside the square, making notes on all the different types of animals they see inside the ring. They should note the movements, habits, or behaviors of any animals (ants, grasshoppers, caterpillars, worms) as they travel (jump, crawl, slither) through the ring. Encourage youngsters to visit their "rings" frequently over a period of several weeks.

5. The following activity helps children appreciate the value of camouflage to animals such as salamanders.

   Obtain 100 green party toothpicks and 100 red toothpicks and a stopwatch or watch. Work with one or more children and mix all the toothpicks together and spread them out on an area of lawn or grass approximately 25 x 25 feet. Give youngsters a time limit (one minute, two minutes, four minutes) to pick up as many toothpicks as possible. At the end of the designated period, invite children to note the number of red toothpicks found in comparison with the number of green toothpicks found. Invite youngsters to speculate on the reasons for different totals.

   You may wish to explain to youngsters that they probably found more red toothpicks than green ones because the green toothpicks were closer to the color of the test area. Thus animals that are able to blend with their surroundings have a better chance of survival. Animals who have distinctive colors may be at a disadvantage.

Art

1. Invite youngsters to create wanted posters for some of the animals in the book. What information should be included on each poster? What vital statistics would students want to share with others via their posters? If possible, obtain one or more wanted posters from your local post office and use them as models for your students' posters.

Math

1. Invite students to develop charts and graphs that record the number of species of each of the animals described in the book. Which species has the greatest number of members around the world? Which has the fewest number of members? Based on the numbers alone, which species is in greatest danger of being placed on an endangered-species list?

Music

1. Youngsters may be surprised to discover the wide variety of animal sounds in their neighborhood. You can assist them in discovering those sounds as follows:

   Provide an inexpensive tape recorder that has a microphone attached with a cord. Invite the child to tape the microphone handle to the end of a broom handle or a long pole (be sure no tape covers the microphone itself). Encourage the child to go outside on a clear and calm day (no wind blowing, for example) and place the microphone near one or more wildlife homes (a bird's nest, a beehive, a wasp's nest [Be Careful!]). The child may wish to check first to be sure the animal(s) are home.

   The child can either hold the microphone on the pole near the animal's home or stick the pole into the ground. It's important to take care not to disturb the animal or its dwelling. Invite the youngster to turn on the microphone and record the noises or sounds the animal makes over a preselected time period.

Social Studies

1. Invite students to post a large map of the world on one wall of the classroom. Encourage them to print the names of the animals in this book on individual index cards and post the cards around the perimeter of the map. They can use lengths of yarn to attach each animal to its country or region of origin. As students learn about other "clever camouflagers," invite them to add those animals to the map.

2. People in this country live in a wide variety of houses or dwellings. Invite children to obtain a journal or notebook and keep an ongoing record of the different types of dwellings. They may wish to take a field trip through their own neighborhood or town or conduct some research in the school or public library. For example, they may wish to construct a chart similar to the following and add to it over an extended period of time:

Dwelling	Where Found	Distinctive Features
Apartment		
Mobile home		
Condo		
Ranch		
Log cabin		
Hut		
Tree house		

3. Invite youngsters to create another chart and investigate the wide variety of dwellings used by animals and the kinds of animals that inhabit each. They may wish to use some of the following examples and add to the list through their library readings: Nest, burrow, cave, tunnel, branch, ledge.

4. Invite students to discuss the similarities between human dwellings and animal homes. What are some of the things that determine where an animal lives? Are those conditions or features similar to the considerations of humans in selecting a living site? Do animals have more options for living spaces than humans?

5. Provide children with drawing materials or (if possible) a camera. Take a walking trip around the neighborhood or across a playground or field. Invite children to note the different types of animal homes they see. Instruct them to be especially watchful and not take anything for granted (for example, an ant hole, a pile of leaves, a bird's nest). Encourage them to take photographs or make drawings of each of those dwellings. After the trip, children can group the animal homes into one or more categories (group homes, homes for individual animals, temporary homes, permanent homes, underground homes, above-ground homes, well-protected homes, homes with special features, etc.). Invite children to share and discuss the similarities and differences they note in their photos and illustrations. This can be an ongoing project lasting several months (youngsters could compare summer homes with winter homes, for example).

Physical Education

1. The book refers to the game of hide-and-seek. Invite students to create their own version of hide-and-seek in which selected students take on the roles of certain designated animals and hide from other members of the class.

From *The Integrated Curriculum, Second Edition.* © 1998 Anthony D. Fredericks. Teacher Ideas Press. (800) 237-6124.

Dear Mr. Henshaw
Beverly Cleary
New York: Morrow, 1983

Summary

Leigh Botts writes to his favorite book author. His letters are filled with questions and advice as well as a lot of revealing information about Leigh's life, his thoughts, and his feelings about his mother and father. This is a touching tale, told strictly through the correspondence of one boy, that offers a realistic and humorous look at the struggles of growing up. The book won the Newbery Award in 1984.

Critical Thinking Questions

1. Why do you think Leigh wrote so many letters to a book author?

2. Why would he want to tell things about his family to a person he had never met?

3. What author would you like to correspond with? Why?

4. How is Leigh's life similar to or different from yours? Is Leigh someone you would like to know?

5. What kinds of questions would you like to ask Beverly Cleary (the author of this book)?

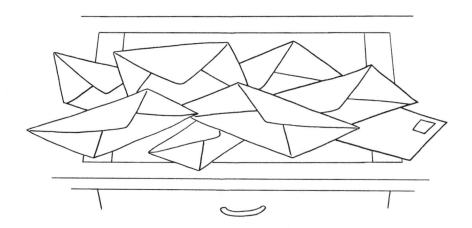

Reading/Language Arts

1. Students will certainly enjoy reading other books by Beverly Cleary. Although there are many, here are a few to get them started: *Henry and Beezus* (New York: Morrow, 1952); *Mitch and Amy* (New York: Morrow, 1967); *Ramona the Pest* (New York: Morrow, 1968); and *Ramona Quimby, Age 8* (New York: Morrow, 1981).

2. Encourage students to read about the life and writings of Beverly Cleary. Your school or local librarian will be able to supply several references. One particularly useful source is the author's own story: *A Girl from Yamhill* (New York: Morrow, 1988).

3. Invite students to put together a guidebook entitled "How to Become a Better Writer." They can interview adults, teachers, businesspeople, reporters, and other children in the community on strategies that help people write. They can assemble their information into a booklet to be distributed to other classes.

4. Students may enjoy setting up a pen pal network with students in another school. Contact colleagues in other schools or contact the education department of a local college and ask for the names of former students who have secured teaching positions in other parts of the state. Contact these individuals and invite their class to correspond with the students in your class and vice versa. Encourage students to keep the letters flowing throughout the year (and beyond!).

5. Invite students to prepare a letter to Beverly Cleary, commenting on this book or any other she has written. Students may wish to include questions about the writing of children's books or about writing in general. Send the letter in care of Ms. Cleary's publisher (William Morrow and Co., 105 Madison Ave., New York, NY 10016). Advise students that since she receives so much mail they may not receive a personal reply, but there's certainly no harm in trying. (By the way, Beverly Cleary's birthday is April 12—students may wish to send her a birthday card).

Science/Health

1. Like Leigh, students may enjoy creating their own electronic gadgets. Various kits can be obtained at your local Radio Shack store. For students interested in constructing their own burglar alarm, *Natural Science Industries* produces the Electro-Tech Kit (available through science catalogs), which allows children to create a variety of electrical objects. A fascinating book for kids is *The X-Ray Picture Book of Everyday Things and How They Work* by Peter Turvey (New York: Watts, 1995).

2. Students will certainly be interested in watching the development and growth of butterflies. Nasco (901 Janesville Ave., Fort Atkinson, WI 53538 [1-800-558-9595]) produces the *Butterfly Garden*, which can be ordered through its catalog or found in many toy and hobby stores. Students will be able to observe and record the growth of butterflies from cocoons to adults.

Art

1. Invite students to put together an oversized collage of trucks and the trucking industry. Using pictures from old magazines as well as information and brochures collected from local trucking firms, students can assemble an informative collage for posting in the classroom or on a wall of the school.

Math

1. Invite students to compute the number of miles from Leigh's home in Pacific Grove, California, to some of the other cities mentioned in the book (e.g., Bakersfield, CA; Taft, CA; Albuquerque, NM; Hermiston, OR). Later, invite students to figure out the number of miles between each of those cities and their school. These figures can be posted on a large classroom map of the United States.

2. Invite students to contact local trucking firms and ask for the number of miles (or number of hours) their drivers are allowed to cover within a 24-hour period. With that data, students can figure out all the cities that can be reached from their town if a driver were to stay within the designated parameters. What towns could Leigh's father drive to (from Pacific Grove, CA) with the time and distance restrictions?

Music

1. Invite students to check the audio sections of their local library or college library for recordings or songs dealing with trucks or truck drivers (country-western songs might be a logical place to begin). Invite students to put together a listing or series of recordings of trucking songs to share with classmates. What is distinctive about these songs?

Social Studies

1. Students may be interested in obtaining travel and tourist information about California. They can write to: Office of Tourism, Box 189, Sacramento, CA 95812-0189. When material arrives, they should arrange it into an attractive display.

2. Students may be interested in putting together a large mural on the history of transportation in this country. Several teams of students could each work in gathering the necessary research for one aspect of transportation (land, air, sea). Information, pictures, brochures, photos, and the like can all be posted on the mural, which can be displayed in the school library.

3. Invite a social worker or psychologist to your classroom to talk about the nature of divorce (please be sensitive to the experiences of your students). The visitor can explain some of the statistics about divorce in this country and discuss the implications for family members. How to deal with divorce and its ramifications can also be part of the presentation. Encourage students to ask questions.

Physical Education

1. Invite students to put together a series of activities or exercises that would be appropriate for truck drivers. Students may wish to interview truck drivers to find out what parts of their bodies they use most and how they maintain some degree of physical conditioning. Are there exercises (isometric) that can be done while driving? Are there activities truckers could practice while not on the road? Students should keep in mind that both men and women are truck drivers and need to maintain appropriate physical conditioning.

Jeremy Thatcher, Dragon Hatcher
Bruce Coville
New York: Simon & Schuster, 1991

Summary

Jeremy purchases a dragon—not just any dragon but one that gets him into all kinds of unimaginable trouble with his friends and family. This is a riotous tale by a master storyteller that will keep young readers asking for more.

Critical Thinking Questions

1. What surprised you most about the owner of the magic shop?

2. Would you have purchased the dragon for the same reasons Jeremy did?

3. What were some of the most memorable scenes in this book?

4. What made this book particularly humorous for you?

5. If you could own any kind of imaginary pet, what would it be?

6. How is Jeremy's personality similar to or different from your personality?

Reading/Language Arts

1. Here are some other books by Bruce Coville that your students will definitely enjoy: *Aliens Ate My Homework, I Left My Sneakers in Dimension X, My Teacher Is an Alien, My Teacher Fried My Brains, Jennifer Murdley's Toad, The Monster's Ring, Space Brat*, and *My Teacher Flunked the Planet*.

2. At the end of the story the dragon, Tiamat, enters a new world. Invite students to write a letter to Tiamat in her new world. They may wish to inquire about where she lives, her friends, and whether she thinks about Jeremy. Provide opportunities for students to share their letters with each other.

3. The author included an epilogue in the book. Invite students to create their own epilogue. What would they include? How would their ending be different from the author's? What important facts would they want to share about Jeremy, his friends, or Tiamat in the last two or three pages of the book?

4. Jeremy got the name for his dragon from a list of great dragons he had made at the library. Invite students to create their own list of dragon names. Which one would they choose if they were naming a dragon?

---

5. Invite students to create their own dragon books. Encourage each student to trace an outline of a dragon on a sheet of construction paper and cut it out. Students may then trace that shape on another piece of construction paper and on several sheets of newsprint and cut them out. All the sheets can be put together (with the construction paper sheets on the front and back) and stapled together. Invite students to write about their favorite dragon on the pages of their "dragon book."

6. Invite students to become reporters who have been transported to the time and place of the book. Encourage them to prepare a newspaper article on an event that happened or a specific incident involving Tiamat.

7. Encourage students to create an original dragon dictionary. Invite them to collect dragon-related words from various books and resources and compile those words into a dictionary (cut in the shape of a dragon).

8. Invite students to write a story about what their town or neighborhood would be like if a dragon lived there. How would the people have to adjust? What would they have to do differently?

Science/Health

1. Invite students to create a manual on the care and feeding of dragons. What kinds of information should they include in the manual? Who would be the audience for the manual—kids or adults? How should they organize the manual? Invite students to look at guidebooks on the care and feeding of various pets (any pet store will have these in stock) and note the types of information included in those books.

2. Invite students to compare Jeremy's dragon with a real life dragon—the Komodo lizard of Indonesia. Students may wish to consult library books about reptiles to obtain information about this giant lizard and its habits. Encourage students to construct a Venn diagram on a bulletin board that illustrates the features and characteristics of dragons versus Komodo lizards.

3. Tiamat kept losing her teeth. Invite a dentist or dental hygienist to your classroom to talk with students about proper dental care. How often should children brush their teeth and what are the proper procedures for brushing? Students may wish to create a "dental care for dragons" booklet based on their learnings.

4. Provide small groups of children with a pile of chicken bones (the bones can be boiled in a solution of water and vinegar and dried thoroughly). Invite each group to arrange the bones into a configuration that would simulate a dragon skeleton. As a further extension (for an extended activity), obtain a copy of *Make Your Own Dinosaur out of Chicken Bones* by Chris McGowan (New York: HarperCollins, 1997). Students may wish to create an "original" dragon skeleton based on the Apatosaurus described in this book.

5. Invite several students to pretend to be dragons and describe their bodies—size, configuration, dimensions, skeletal structure, and other important features. Invite each one to explain why his or her (dragon) body is different from those of other creatures. (It may be necessary to precede this activity with one in which each student describes his or her body.)

6. Encourage students to create their own dragon "fossils." Provide small groups of students with pie plates half filled with wet sand. Invite each group to place several chicken bones in the sand. Circular strips of cardboard can be placed around the bones and plaster of paris mixed and poured into the makeshift molds. After the plaster of paris has dried, encourage students to examine their "fossils" to note any distinguishing features or characteristics.

Art

1. Jeremy was an artist, yet the book does not contain an abundance of illustrations. Invite students to create their own illustrations for some of their favorite scenes in the book. Which scenes should definitely be illustrated and which scenes should best be left to the imagination of the reader?

2. Provide students with empty shoe boxes, various pieces of colored construction paper, glue, scissors, and other art materials. Invite students (individually or in small groups) to design dioramas of selected scenes from the book.

Math

1. Invite students to research the wingspans of various birds. Encourage them to create a comparative chart of wingspans from the smallest (the Helena hummingbird—3 inches) to the largest (the wandering albatross—$10\frac{1}{2}$ feet). Invite students to predict Tiamat's wingspan and place her on the appropriate place on the chart.

2. Jeremy normally played a game of baseball at recess time. You may wish to conduct a short lesson on how baseball players' batting averages are computed (number of hits divided by number of times at bat). Invite students to play several games of baseball or softball and to keep running records of each player's batting averages over an extended period of time.

Music

1. If possible, obtain a recording of "Puff the Magic Dragon" (a popular folk song by Peter, Paul, and Mary recorded in the 1960s). Play the song for students and invite them to discuss the similarities between Puff and Tiamat. Encourage students to create an original song or song lyrics for Tiamat.

Social Studies

1. Invite students to conduct some library research on famous dragons in folktales and other forms of traditional literature. Students may wish to compare and contrast dragons that appear in Chinese folktales and those that appear in traditional English literature, for example. Invite students to assemble a guidebook entitled "Notable Dragons in Literature." In which countries do/did most dragons live? Invite students to post a large wall map and indicate the location of stories, tales, and legends about well-known dragons throughout history.

Physical Education

1. Invite students to play a game of baseball (see Math #2 above). Invite students to discuss Olympic track and field events that are "embedded" in the game. For example, running (foot races), leaping (high jump), throwing (javelin, shot put), and executing a double play (relays). Encourage students to compile a list of comparative sports.

More Scary Stories to Tell in the Dark
Alvin Schwartz
New York: Harper & Row, 1984

Summary

People who take the form of cats, hands dangling inside the closet, strange disappearances and reappearances, corpses, goblins, and ghosts all haunt this collection of scary stories and frightful tales. The emphasis is on fright, and the stories retold in this book offer young readers a potpourri of possible campfire, slumber party, and after-class tales to share and enjoy.

Critical Thinking Questions

1. Which of the stories was the scariest? What made it so scary?

2. What elements does a scary story have to have?

3. Do you know any stories that are scarier than the stories in this book? Can you share one with us?

4. Which one of these stories do you think would make a good movie? Why?

5. Is there anything in your life that could be included in a collection of scary stories? Can you describe it for us?

Reading/Language Arts

1. Students will enjoy reading other scary and ghost stories. Introduce them to books such as *Famous Ghost Stories* by Bennett Cerf (New York: Random House, 1944); *Things That Go Bump in the Night* by Louis Jones (New York: Hill & Wang, 1959); *The Thing at the Foot of the Bed and Other Scary Stories* by Maria Leach (New York: World, 1959); and *Scary Stories to Tell in the Dark* by Alvin Schwartz (New York: Lippincott, 1981).

2. Have students write a letter to one of the characters in the book. Which character would they choose—a protagonist or a victim? Why did they choose that particular individual?

3. Have students work in small groups to rewrite one of the stories in the book. Their version, however, will include the names of classmates and locations in their community. Provide opportunities for students to share their stories in written or oral form.

4. Assemble a group of six to eight students. Ask one student to begin telling a scary story; however, he or she only has three minutes. At the end of the three minutes the story is continued by the next person, who also has three minutes. The process continues until everyone has a chance to contribute to the story with the last person devising an appropriate ending (scary, of course).

Science/Health

1. Many scary stories rely on one's knowledge of human anatomy. You may wish to invite a professor from a local college to give your students a quick lesson on human anatomy with particular reference to hands, brains, hearts, and other body parts that tend to appear most in these types of stories. An excellent supplemental film (which has won many awards) is *Man: The Incredible Machine* (Washington, DC: National Geographic Society, 1975 [catalog no. 51255]).

2. Students may be interested in creating a small sample of fog. Obtain a large-mouth jar and a margarine container. Fill the jar half way with very warm water. Put the margarine container in the mouth of the jar (it may need to be sealed with paraffin or petroleum jelly). Fill the margarine container with ice cubes. Have students observe what happens inside the jar. Depending on the room temperature of the classroom, either a small cloud, some fog, or lots of water droplets will form inside the jar. Students should experiment with different water temperatures and room temperatures to create the best conditions for "manufacturing" fog.

3. Cats are a popular animal in many scary stories. Have students conduct some research on the behavior and characteristics of cats. They may wish to assemble their data into a descriptive scrapbook for classroom display.

4. Students may wish to construct their own models of a human skeleton. One version, a scientifically accurate skeleton assembled from die-cut cardboard sheets, is available from Albion Import Export Co., Coolidge Bank Bldg., 65 Main St., Watertown, MA 02172. Another version, slightly less expensive, is produced by Lindberg and can be found in most toy and hobby stores.

Art

1. Have students work in small groups to design an illustration of their favorite story. They may wish to use the illustrations in the book as prototypes or create their own.

2. Have students put together a collage of a haunted house. Using pictures from old magazines and a large sheet of construction paper, students can "build" a haunted house to their own specifications.

Math

1. The story "The Bad News" deals with baseball. Have students compute the batting averages of some of their favorite baseball players. The statistics are usually printed in most daily newspapers, including times at bat and number of hits. With those two figures students can compute batting averages and check them against the figures reported in the newspaper.

---

2. In "Wonderful Sausage" various individuals are turned into sausage. Have students research the prices of various types of sausage in their local community and prepare a comparative chart listing all the prices and the varieties available. Have students compute prices for various weights (such as the equivalent weights of classmates) of sausage at various stores.

3. Most scary stories take place at night. Have students compute (and chart) the length of the night (from the exact time of sunset to the exact time of sunrise) at various times during the year. Figures can be converted into hours, minutes, and seconds.

Music

1. Have students check with the music teacher or with their friends to obtain various sound-effects records. Have them put together a recording of sounds and songs that would be appropriate for one or more stories in this book.

Social Studies

1. Students may be interested in the history of ghost stories or scary tales from other countries. Have them conduct some library research and make a presentation on the stories that we tell in this country as well as stories that are popular in other countries. Some books to get them started include *Haunted England: A Survey of English Ghostlore* by Christina Hole (London: B. T. Batsford, 1950) and *Legends of the City of Mexico* by Thomas Janvier (New York: Harper, 1910).

2. Invite students to write a biographical sketch of a ghost. Introduce students to biographies of famous people and the chronology of events in those stories. Have students create their own biographies of scary creatures—real or imagined.

3. Ask students to look into the Salem witch trials and the controversy that surrounds that period of American history. Ask students to prepare a brochure on the witch trials for sharing with other classes.

4. Contact a local or regional folklore society in your area and invite one of its storytellers to visit your classroom to share some tales. Have the individual share some of the history behind the stories told as well as information on their origins.

Physical Education

1. Have students conduct races without using some parts of their anatomy. For example, have students race a course with their hands tied behind their backs. Have students conduct races without using their legs (use the scooters available from the PE teacher). Or have students conduct races while blindfolded (use extreme caution). Challenge students to invent other types of races in which one or more body parts cannot be used.

My Side of the Mountain
Jean Craighead George
New York: Dutton, 1988

Summary

Sam Gribley is tired of living in a crowded New York City apartment, so he runs away to the Catskill Mountain wilderness to forge a life of his own. He must rely on his ingenuity and on the resources of the land to survive.

Critical Thinking Questions

1. Are you brave enough to go off on your own and live in the wilderness?

2. What types of things would you bring along to help you survive in the wilderness?

3. Why do you think Sam disliked New York City so much?

4. If you were Sam, what would you have done differently?

5. Do you think Frightful's parents missed him as much as Sam's parents did?

Reading/Language Arts

1. Here are some additional related titles that students will enjoy reading: *Bears on Hemlock Mountain* by Alice Dalgleish (New York: Aladdin, 1981); *Deep in the Forest* by Brinton Turkle (New York: E. P. Dutton, 1981); *Once I Was Scared* by Helena Claret Pittman (New York: Puffin, 1993); *Caught in the Moving Mountains* by Gloria Skurzynski (New York: Beech Tree, 1994); *Incident at Hawk's Hill* by Allan W. Eckert (Boston: Little Brown, 1995); and *The Cay* by Theodore Taylor (New York: Doubleday, 1987).

2. Invite students to maintain a diary over an extended time period (a week, a month). What events occur on a frequent basis? What events occur only once? If someone found a student's diary, what would they be able to learn about that individual's life?

Science/Health

1. Students may enjoy making some rock candy using the following recipe:

   Pour ½ cup water into a saucepan and bring it to a boil. Add about a cup of sugar to the water, spoonful by spoonful, stirring so that the sugar completely dissolves. Keep adding the sugar until you have a clear syrup. Take care that the syrup doesn't boil over. Let the syrup cool for about ten minutes before carefully pouring it into a glass. Tie a piece of string to a pencil. Tie a paper clip to the other end of the string and lay the pencil on the glass so the paper clip just touches the bottom of the glass. It will take about a week for crystals to form along the string. Invite students to check the glass every day, carefully breaking any crust that forms on the top of the syrup, to allow evaporation to continue. The less the solution is disturbed, the better the crystal formation will be. Students may wish to chart the growth of the crystals in a journal or notebook.

2. Encourage students to assemble a leaf scrapbook. Invite students to collect several examples of different leaves in and around the school and mount each leaf on a separate sheet of paper. Invite students to research each leaf in the school or public library to determine the type of tree it came from and all its distinguishing characteristics.

3. Provide students with a random assortment of several kinds of vegetable seeds. Encourage them to plant each one in some potting soil (fill the empty compartments of an egg carton three-quarters full with potting soil and moisten lightly). Before each seed sprouts, invite students to make some guesses as to what each will become. After the seeds have germinated, allow students to transplant them outside into a small garden, if possible.

4. Sam met many animals in the story. Encourage students to conduct some library research on animals that hibernate in winter. Why do animals hibernate? What do they do for food and water? Encourage students to select an animal mentioned in the story.

Art

1. Ask students how they think nature has influenced art over the years. If possible, take students to a local museum or art gallery to look at paintings and drawings that represent things in nature. If a museum is not nearby, take students to the local public library and ask for books of prints representing artists that traditionally paint nature scenes (for example, Frederic Church, Claude Monet). Which paintings might be representative of the environment in which Sam lived?

2. Students may wish to make a corn necklace using Indian corn or other large-kernel corn. Thread a needle and "sew" the kernels on the thread one by one (the kernels may need to be soaked in water for several hours before sewing). After sufficient kernels are on the string, tie the ends together to form a necklace. Dry in the sun or a slow oven (250 degrees).

Math

1. Students can make some potpourri with almost anything that grows in nature. Fragrant herbs, spices, and flowers are used to perfume the mixture. They can also use dried herbs and spices from the kitchen. A variety of interesting combinations can be tried. Here's one to get you started:

 ### *Rambling Rose*

3 c. dried rose petals	1 tbsp. ground allspice
2 c. dried lavender	1 tbsp. ground cinnamon
1 c. dried lemon verbena	1 tbsp. ground cloves
1 tbsp. dried lemon peel	1½ tbsp. ground orn's root

Mix together the last five ingredients before adding the herbs and flowers. Stir well.

- -

Invite students to experiment with different quantities and amounts of selected ingredients. What is the overall effect on the quality of the finished product? For example, if they doubled the amount of rose petals and halved the amount of cloves, how would the final product differ?

Music

1. Invite students to assemble a collection of "wilderness" music as well as a collection of "city" music (country and western music might be an appropriate place to start). What elements of each are similar? What elements are distinctive to each geographical area?

Social Studies

1. Invite students to imagine they are living in the wild and are writing to a friend to convince him or her to visit for several days. What features or attractions should be pointed out in the letter? Afterward, invite students to imagine they are in the city and writing to a friend who lives in the wild—inviting that person for a visit.

2. Obtain one or more topological maps of your state from the public library or geography department of a local college. Divide the class into several groups and invite each group to plot the location of wilderness areas on the map. Invite each group to identify how those areas are similar to or different from the one in which Sam lived.

3. Invite students to prepare a description of their local area from the perspective of an inanimate object. For example, if they live in an urban area, how would that area look from the viewpoint of a factory? If they live in a suburban area, how would that area look from the viewpoint of a stop sign? How would a rural area look from the viewpoint of a pine tree?

4. Invite students to create a videotaped walking or automobile tour of your town or area. Students may wish to design a route that includes major highlights of the area and write appropriate narration for inclusion on the videotape. These productions can be shared with students in other classes.

Physical Education

1. Invite students to put together an informational book on exercises appropriate for living in the wild. What type of conditioning routine would be useful in order to maintain top physical shape?

2. Invite someone from a local hiking or orienteering club (check your local phone book) to visit the class and discuss some of the physical skills necessary for the sport. How do club members stay in shape? What exercises do they do on a regular basis?

Sadako and the Thousand Paper Cranes

Eleanor Coerr

New York: Putnam, 1977

Summary

Sadako was two years old when the atom bomb was dropped on Hiroshima. Although she was not injured during the bomb attack, she became ill with leukemia ten years later. A friend told Sadako that if she folded a thousand paper cranes, they would bring her good luck and she would live a long life. Sadako died before she could fold all the cranes, but her classmates folded the remainder, and they were buried with Sadako.

Critical Thinking Questions

1. Which of Sadako's qualities did you especially admire? In what ways is Sadako like you?

2. How did you feel immediately after reading this book? How do you think your best friend would feel?

3. Why do you think the author wanted to write this book? Did she have any particular message?

4. If you had an opportunity to say anything to Sadako before she died, what would you have said?

Reading/Language Arts

1. This book talks about several good-luck signs. Invite students to create an original good-luck charm and write a paragraph to go with it. They can write the paragraph in the form of the daily horoscope column in the newspaper.

2. Encourage students to read the book *The Faithful Elephants* by Yukion Tsuchiya (Boston: Houghton Mifflin, 1988). Invite students to summarize the story from an animal's viewpoint.

3. Students may be interested in reading books about the human body. Here are a few to get them started: *Blood and Guts: A Working Guide to Your Own Insides* by Linda Allen (Boston: Little, Brown, 1976); *Our Bodies* by Robert Brown (Milwaukee, WI: Gareth Stevens, 1990); *The Body Atlas* by Mark Crocker (New York: Oxford University Press, 1991); *Outside and Inside You* by Sandra Markle (New York: Bradbury Press, 1991); and *The Human Body and How It Works* by Angela Royston (New York: Random House, 1990).

Science/Health

1. If possible, seek permission to visit a local physical rehabilitation center or chiropractor. Encourage students to talk with the personnel about the structure and function of the human skeleton and muscle system. How can we protect our bones and muscles? What are some possible exercises and dietary habits? What happens to people who suffer diseases or injuries to their bones or muscles? On your return to the classroom, invite students to collect the information into a brochure to be shared with other classes.

2. The human skeleton continues to grow until sometime between the ages of 16 and 22. Invite students to record the heights of their family members and repeat the measurements once each month. Encourage students to make predictions about each family member's height for the forthcoming month. Which persons in the family are continuing to grow? Who has stopped growing? Students may wish to create a special chart or graph of family members' heights over time. Friends and other relatives can be added to the chart, too.

3. Here are two excellent videos about the human body to share with students: *The Incredible Human Machine* and *The Invisible World* (catalog nos. 50873 and 51595, respectively, National Geographic Society, Washington, DC 20036).

4. Invite the school nurse or a local doctor to visit the class and talk to students about the importance of good health. Prior to the speaker's arrival, invite students to compile a list of questions they would like to ask. Set up a video camera and videotape the speaker's presentation for review at a later date. Encourage students to compare the information the speaker(s) shares with data from other sources.

5. Assign each of several groups a specific human disease. Challenge each group to locate as much outside information as possible about the causes of and cures for each selected illness. Invite groups to assemble their data in the form of brochures or leaflets that can be distributed throughout the school. Local health organizations can be contacted for some preliminary data.

6. Select one or more of the following field trips to share with children. Depending on the size and location of your local community, additional visits to other sites (with accompanying interviews) may also be possible. Check with your local health organization, hospital, doctor referral service, or visiting-nurses association. They will be glad to refer you to additional groups, organizations, and specialists.

    a. If possible, visit a nearby blood bank and encourage youngsters to talk with one of the technicians or nurses. Invite them to find out how blood is collected, measured, stored, and preserved. What precautions do the workers have to follow? How much blood is collected in a day, a week, or a month? How is that blood used?

    b. If possible, make arrangements to visit the emergency room of a local hospital. Invite students to prepare questions to ask emergency room technicians, nurses, or doctors about some of the typical cases they treat during the course of a week. Upon returning to the classroom, invite students to prepare a descriptive brochure on what they learned.

Art

1. Work with students to make a map of Japan using burlap. Cut a large piece of blue burlap to serve as the base and to represent the ocean. Cut another piece of burlap in a different color in the shape of the island of Japan. Invite students to make a key and sew symbols on the map with yarn and simple stitches. Include bodies of water, large cities, lines of latitude and longitude. Sew the island to the base, leaving an opening of 4 inches. Stuff a thin layer of polyester fiberfill into the pocket between the island and the base (this will give the map a 3-D effect). Sew the opening shut.

2. Provide opportunities for students to make paper cranes and suspend them from the ceiling. Use the book *The Magic of Origami* by Alice Gray and Kunihiko Kasahara (New York: Japan Publishing, 1977, pp. 84–85) for an example. Other origami books include *Easy Origami* by Dokwhteli Nakano (New York: Viking, 1985) and *Paper Magic: The Art of Paper Folding* by Robert Harbin (Boston: Newton, 1957).

Math

1. Students may enjoy making this popular Japanese dish:

✂ *Black and White Salad*

(this recipe makes enough for four people)

INGREDIENTS

4–6 leftover boiled potatoes	1 can cooked mussels
pinch of dill	salt and pepper
2 tbsp. white vinegar	1 can button mushrooms
mace	parsley (large handful)
juice from ½ lemon	walnut halves

DIRECTIONS

Slice potatoes. Mix next four ingredients and marinate potatoes in the mixture. Add a pinch of dill and a little powdered mace. Drain the mussels and the mushrooms. Mix gently with potatoes. Garnish with a few walnut halves.

 -·

After students have made the recipe, invite them to calculate the quantities of ingredients that would be necessary to make enough for 20 people, 65 people, everybody at your grade level, or any other large group of people.

Music

1. Work with the music teacher to put together a collection of traditional Japanese music to share with students. Invite students to note some of the distinctive qualities or characteristics of traditional Japanese music and how it differs from traditional western music.

2. Invite students to select a song or tune that would be appropriate to play while reading this story out loud (see #1) to another group of students. Is there a song that would capture the tone or mood of the story without interfering with its theme?

Social Studies

1. Obtain photocopies of major newspapers from 1945 reporting the drop of the bomb and its effects (a local college library or newspaper company could supply these). Invite students to use this information to write a radio announcement reporting the event. If possible, encourage students to record the announcements onto a tape recorder.

2. Invite students to interview grandparents or a special older friend about what was happening during their lives at the time of the bomb, how the war changed their lives, and how they felt about the war and the dropping of the bomb. Be sure to provide opportunities for students to share that information.

3. Invite students to write to several travel agencies to get information about a trip to Japan. Students can ask about different ways to get there and the associated costs, types of accommodations and whether meals are included in the price, the availability of guided tours, etc. Encourage students to make a chart comparing the information from the agencies.

4. Sadako was taken to a Red Cross hospital. Students may want to visit a local office of the American Red Cross. Ask for information about what the Red Cross does and how citizens can help.

Physical Education

1. If possible, obtain permission to visit a local rehabilitation center or chiropractor. Encourage students to talk with the personnel about the structure and function of the human skeleton and muscle system. The data that students collect can be assembled into a scrapbook or notebook.

Tales of a Fourth Grade Nothing
Judy Blume
New York: Dutton, 1972

Summary

Life with an energetic two-year-old brother can be exasperating for nine-year-old Peter. "Fudge" has tantrums, wrecks Peter's schoolwork, breaks his teeth trying to fly, and creates general mayhem.

Critical Thinking Questions

1. Why do you think Peter's little brother is nicknamed Fudge?

2. How would you feel if you lost a pet? Do you think Peter has the same feelings? Why?

3. If you could spend a day with Peter in New York, what are some things you would like to do?

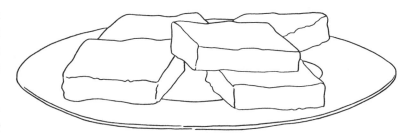

4. Do you think the title is appropriate for the story? Why?

5. What would Peter's life would be like without Fudge?

Reading/Language Arts

1. Invite students to look through the classified section of your local newspaper. Based on examples in the newspaper, challenge students to create an original classified advertisement based on their favorite part of the book. For example:

> FOR SALE cheap: Little brother, cries without reason. Messes up stuff in bedroom. Good for lots of laughs. $50.00 or best offer. Available immediately. Call Peter at 123-4567 after 4:00 P.M.

Science/Health

1. Invite students to determine (through guessing or actual counting) how many teeth they have in their mouths. Based on that number, encourage students to determine the number of teeth in the entire class. Discuss with students reasons for good dental care. How should one brush his or her teeth? How often? What other forms of dental care should be practiced in addition to daily brushing? For educational material contact American Dental Association, Order Department, 211 E. Chicago Ave., Chicago, IL 60611, or call 800-621-8099, ext. 2639.

2. Students may be interested in reading some books about turtles. Here are a few to get them started: *Turtle Day* by Douglas Florian (New York: Crowell, 1989); *Box Turtle at Long Pond* by William George (New York: Greenwillow Books, 1989); *Lily Pad Pond* by Bianca Lavies (New York: Dutton, 1989); *At the Frog Pond* by Tilde Michels (New York: Lippincott, 1989); and *Turtle in July* by Marilyn Singer (New York: Macmillan, 1989).

Art

1. Students may enjoy making some Pretzel Turtles. Here's a simple recipe:

✂ *Pretzel Turtles*

INGREDIENTS

1 package yeast	4½ c. flour
1½ c. warm water	1 egg yolk
(105–115 degrees)	2 tbsp. water
½ tsp. sugar	coarse salt or sesame seeds

DIRECTIONS

Dissolve the package of yeast with the warm water and add sugar. Add flour and knead for 5–6 minutes. Let the covered dough rise in a greased bowl until doubled in size. Divide the dough into 12 pieces and shape into turtles. Blend together the egg yolk and the 2 tablespoons water and brush some of the mixture on the pretzels. Sprinkle the salt or sesame seeds on each pretzel. Place on a cookie sheet. Bake at 450 degrees for 12 minutes. Yield: 12 pretzels.

✂ -

Math

1. Students may also enjoy preparing some no-cook fudge in honor of Fudgie. Here's a recipe:

✂ *Fudge*

INGREDIENTS

9 c. sugar	2 c. margarine (four sticks)
½ c. cocoa (no sugar)	2 tsp. vanilla extract
	¾ c. peanut butter

DIRECTIONS

Stir the sugar and cocoa together in a medium-sized bowl. Melt the margarine very slowly. Add margarine, peanut butter, and vanilla to the sugar and cocoa mixture and mix well. Spread onto one large greased pan (9½ x 11). Refrigerate until firm and cut into small squares.

✂ -

Invite students to alter or change the measurements of the selected ingredients. What happens to the final product? Then invite students to determine the quantities of ingredients necessary so that everyone in the class gets a piece or so that everyone in the school gets a piece.

Music

1. Provide opportunities for students to use their own instruments and create a musical theme for Fudgie. They may wish to listen to some of the theme songs used for TV sit-coms. Later, they can record their theme and play it prior to a re-reading of the story.

Social Studies

1. Fudgie certainly did not have the best manners in the world. Sometimes he was even downright embarrassing and rude. Invite students to read the book *What Do You Say, Dear? A Book of Manners for All Occasions* by Sesyle Joslin (New York: Scholastic, 1980). This is a humorous book about manners for younger readers. Invite students to create a list of manners they think Fudgie could have used in the story. Talk with students about the importance of manners in everyday life. Is it equally important for both children and adults to have good manners?

Physical Education

1. Invite students to interview nurses, doctors, physical therapists, or other health care professionals about the level of physical fitness that should be maintained by children their age. What is an average weight or height for students at that grade level? What types of physical activities should students be participating in on a regular basis? Invite students to write a letter to the editor of the local newspaper about the role of physical fitness in the lives or fourth- and fifth-grade students.

Where the Buffaloes Begin
Olaf Baker
New York: Warne, 1981

Summary

Little Wolf, a courageous Indian boy, longs to find the lake described in an Indian legend—the lake where the buffaloes began. In his quest to fulfill that dream, he begins an adventure that ends with an unforgettable ride through the night to save his people.

Critical Thinking Questions

1. Why do some people still perceive Native Americans to be bad people?

2. Would you have liked to live as a Native American in the 1800s? How would life then be different from your life now?

3. How do you think Little Wolf felt when he realized that his people were in danger? Have you ever been in a similar situation or had similar feelings?

4. Do you think Little Wolf should have been punished for leaving the camp without permission? Why?

5. What do you think was the most frightening thing Little Wolf faced? Did he react in the same way you would have reacted? Why or why not?

Reading/Language Arts

1. Discuss sign language as a means of communication. You may wish to teach students a few signs used by Native Americans of the Plains. Many Native American signs can be found in *America's Fascinating Indian Heritage* (Pleasantville, NY: Reader's Digest Association, 1978).

2. Invite students to create and write a character sketch of Little Wolf. What did he look like? What were some of his qualities?

3. Invite students to construct a series of letters they would want to write to Little Wolf. The letters can inquire about Native American life, tribal customs, and typical events in his life. The letters can be "sent" to students in other classes who have read the book and can answer in the "voice" of Little Wolf.

---

4. Students may enjoy reading other books about Native American life including one or more of the following: *Indians of the Northern Plains* by William Powers (New York: Putnams, 1969); *Indians of the Southern Plains* by William Powers (New York: Putnams, 1971); *Indians of the Southwest* by Gordon Baldwin (New York: Putnams, 1970). Invite students to compare the various lifestyles of Native Americans. Students may wish to write about the influence of geography and climate on Native American life.

5. Divide the class into several small groups and invite each group to create an alternate ending for the story. Encourage each group to share its ending with the entire class and decide which ending is most exciting, most plausible, or most dramatic. Students can share their written endings by posting them on the bulletin board.

Science/Health

1. Invite a meteorologist from a local TV station or college to visit your class to explain the nature of wind. What causes wind? How is it measured? How are different wind speeds classified? Students should be prepared to ask questions. Background information can be obtained from books such as *The Usborne Book of Weather Facts* by Anita Ganeri (Tulsa, OK: EDC, 1987); *Air, Light, and Water* by Mary-Jane Wilkins (New York: Random House, 1990); and *Weather* by Brian Cosgrove (New York: Knopf, 1991).

2. Invite students to compile a list of descriptive information about buffalo. How important were buffalo to the lives of the Plains Native Americans? How many uses did they have for buffalo products? What was the life span of a buffalo? Information can be garnered from several sources, including *America's Fascinating Indian Heritage* (Pleasantville, NY: Reader's Digest Association, 1978) and *The Indian and the Buffalo* by Robert Hofsinde (New York: Morrow, 1961).

3. Invite students to read *Corn Is Maize: The Gift of the Indians* by Aliki (New York: Crowell, 1976). Afterward, obtain some packets of corn seed from a local garden center and allow students to grow their own corn plants according to directions on the seed packets. (They can plant two or three seeds to a cup filled with a mixture of potting soil and dirt. Place the cups in a sunny location and water occasionally. If it is springtime, students can plant the seeds outdoors in an appropriate location.) Provide opportunities for students to chart the growth of their corn plants.

4. Students may wish to start a "Native American garden" on the school grounds. Students can consult *The American Indian As Farmer* by Loverne Morris (Chicago: Melmont, 1963) for the appropriate crops. They can also write to several seed companies to obtain catalogs and the necessary seeds for the garden.

Art

1. Check with a local crafts store and obtain several Native American bead kits for your students. Students may wish to create examples of belts and bracelets for display or individual wearing.

2. Provide students with finger paints and paper and invite them to create various paintings of buffalo and buffalo hunts.

Math

1. Invite students to conduct some library research on the dimensions and weight of both the buffalo and an average-sized horse. Encourage students to develop a comparative chart outlining several dimensions of these two animals. Have students discuss any similarities or differences.

2. A typical teepee required approximately 20 buffalo pelts. Encourage students to calculate the number of buffalo pelts needed to house a village of 50 families, 27 families, or 83 families.

3. Invite students to create their own bartering system similar to the one Native Americans used. Encourage students to bring in several items such as a blanket, a pair of shoes, a shirt, and a toy gun. Invite students to establish a "pricing guide" that is not based on money but rather on the estimated worth of those objects. Encourage students to design a "comparative shopping" guide for the trading of common objects.

Music

1. An excellent recording to play for students is *Songs of Earth, Water, Fire, and Sky (Music of the American Indians)* (New York: New World Records, 1976). After students have listened to several selections, invite them to interpret the meanings of those songs. Why did the Native Americans create songs about the forces of nature? What kinds of instruments were used to depict the forces of nature?

Social Studies

1. Divide the class into several groups. Invite each group to select and research a particular Native American tribe, including their lifestyles, where they lived, some of their customs and traditions, whether they were farmers or hunters, and types of dwellings. Each group should be prepared to collect its data into booklet form to be shared with other students in the class.

2. The National Geographic Society (Washington, DC) has an excellent filmstrip series entitled *The Life of the American Indian* (catalog no. 03243, 1977). The two sound filmstrips provide valuable data on the eastern, Plains, northwestern, and southwestern Native Americans of this country. A complementary video (also from the National Geographic Society) is *American Indians: A Brief History* (catalog no. 51004, 1985).

Physical Education

1. Students may wish to play a modern version of the American Indian game Chunkey. In the game, players roll a rimmed disk (a garbage can lid or small patio tabletop would make appropriate substitutes) down a grassy court. Two people run after the disk and throw wooden poles as close as possible to the spot where they expect the disk to fall over. The closest one wins!

The Whipping Boy
Sid Fleischman
New York: Greenwillow Books, 1986

Summary

Jemmy, who must be whipped every time the prince gets into trouble, leads the young highness through the forests and sewers of old England in an adventure filled with suspense, strange characters, and the coming of age of "Prince Brat."

Critical Thinking Questions

1. What would you enjoy most about living during the time Jemmy and Prince Brat did? Why?

2. Is Prince Brat similar to anyone you know? In what ways?

3. What types of adventures do you think the two boys would get into in a sequel to this story?

4. How would Prince Brat's inability to read have been a problem for him later in life?

5. Describe what you would need in order to live in a sewer.

Reading/Language Arts

1. Invite students to suggest some ideas or strategies that would help the young prince learn to read. What do students do during their reading lessons that would be helpful to the prince?

2. Some students may wish to create an imaginary journal that could have been written by the prince (if he could write). Entries could include the various adventures the two youngsters got into, the characters they saw along the way, and how they eventually settled their differences.

3. Encourage several students to write a sequel to the story. What kinds of new adventures would the two young boys get into? Would their friendship blossom or would they fall back into their old familiar ways?

4. Have students check the local yellow pages for the modern-day services that might be used by royalty. Examples may include transportation and carpet-cleaning services (for the red carpet), and agencies that provide butlers and cooks.

---

5. Have students pretend they are news reporters covering the "kidnapping" of the prince. What facts or details would they want to include in a TV broadcast? Which ones would be appropriate for a newspaper article?

Science/Health

1. Have several students investigate the life cycle of one of the animals mentioned in the story (e.g., horse, bear, cow, rat). They can share this information in a poster or an oral report.

2. Have students investigate fog. What is it, how is it created, and what effects does it have on our daily lives?

3. Provide students with small slices of garlic, onion, potato, and apple and ask them to taste each one. What differences or similarities do they note? Afterward, blindfold several students and ask each to hold his or her nose. Give each student slices of the same items as before but in random order. Ask each student to explain why he or she had a difficult time distinguishing between the different items.

4. Some students may enjoy looking into the nutritional needs of various people and animals mentioned in the story. They can assemble this information in a chart that lists the daily nutritional needs of growing children, adults, bears, rats, cows, and horses. What similarities or differences are there among these individuals?

5. Have students investigate differences in sanitation between the time of this story and modern times. Why is sanitation such an important environmental issue?

Art

1. Have students create an animal collage by cutting out various pictures of cows, rats, horses, and bears from nature or environmental magazines. They can attach the pictures to sheets of construction paper and display them throughout the room.

2. Students may wish to create a line of greeting cards that could have been used by characters in the story. For example, what type of card would Billy and Cutwater send to the king? What type of card would the prince want to send his father at the end of the story?

3. Have students create imaginary advertisements for some of the characters at the fair. Have students imagine that each character was going to put an ad in the local newspaper. What information should be included in each ad in order to attract more business?

Math

1. Have students locate various dimensions of the animals mentioned in the story. For example, what is the average weight, length, and height of a rat? This information can be graphed on a sheet of oaktag.

2. Some students may wish to investigate the difference between the English monetary system and the American monetary system. What differences or similarities are there?

3. Bring in a large bag of potatoes and have students practice addition or multiplication facts using potatoes in various arrangements and sets.

4. Ask students to locate current prices on some of the items mentioned in the story. For example, how much does a bar of soap cost? A bag of potatoes? A horse? A clove of garlic? To what can they attribute the variations in prices?

Music

1. Demonstrate for students how various instruments can be used to imitate the motions or movements of various animals. For example, a flute can be used to depict a bird, and a tuba can depict a bear. You may find it helpful to play recordings of "Peter and the Wolf" and "Carnival of the Animals" so that students can hear how different instruments suggest the movements of various animals.

2. Have students create various homemade instruments that could be used in a retelling of the story. For example, two coconut shells pounded on a hard surface would provide the sound of a horse. Two sandpaper blocks rubbed together can imitate the sound of the boys walking slowly through the fog-shrouded forest. Rubbing wet fingers around the rim of a glass could imitate the sound of the sewer rats.

3. Students may enjoy listening to the record *The Lady and the Unicorn* by John Renbourn, Warner Bros.—a collection of medieval music, folk tunes, and early classical music on guitars, sitar, hand-drums, glockenspiel, viola, concertina, flutes, and violin.

Social Studies

1. Have students look up the history of fairs and carnivals. How have they changed over the years? What events at today's fairs are identical to those of fairs of long ago?

2. Direct students to construct an imaginary map of the prince's kingdom. Be sure to have them include all the sites mentioned in the story as well as any others they think would be important in a kingdom.

3. Ask students to interview their parents, grandparents, or relatives on family stories, folktales, or legends that they learned as children. If some families have recently immigrated to this country, you may want to invite children's relatives to class to share some stories and legends from their country of origin.

4. Have students investigate the different types of costumes worn by people during the time of this story. What kinds of clothes did rich people wear? What kinds of clothes were worn by poor people? What differences were there?

5. Ask students to collect several copies of travel magazines and prepare one description of England as it was in the time of this story and another description of England as it exists today. How do these two descriptions compare?

Physical Education

1. Have students invent various activities that would allow someone to stay in shape if he or she had to live in a sewer.

2. Have students imitate some of the body movements of characters at the fair—for example, acrobats, stilt walkers, jugglers.

3. Students may be interested in engaging in some orienteering activities. You should be able to locate several orienteering books at your local library or bookstore.

RECOMMENDED SUPPLEMENTAL CHILDREN'S LITERATURE

The following lists include many books recommended for reluctant readers. These lists are not intended to be definitive or exhaustive; use them as starting points, supplementing them with your own favorites, books recommended by colleagues, literature reviewed in professional journals, and, most important, books that interest your students.

It is my hope that in these books you will discover many possibilities to stimulate and energize all the readers in your classroom. I hope your classroom will be filled with tales, novels, stories, fables, myths, legends, sagas, and fantasies—books of every genre. A classroom that overflows with literature is a classroom that promotes reading as a viable and valuable part of every student's life. Fill your classroom with books and you may fill the mind of even the most reluctant reader with imagination and a sense of discovery and wonder.

Grades 1–2

Ackerman, Karen. *Song and Dance Man*. New York: Knopf, 1988.

Aliki. *Digging Up Dinosaurs*. New York: Crowell, 1988.

———. *We Are Best Friends*. New York: Greenwillow Books, 1982.

Allard, Harry. *The Stupids Step Out*. Boston: Houghton Mifflin, 1974.

Asch, Frank. *Happy Birthday, Moon!* New York: Prentice Hall Press, 1982.

Balian, Lorna. *The Aminal*. New York: Abingdon, 1972.

Bang, Molly. *Ten, Nine, Eight*. New York: Greenwillow Books, 1983.

———. *The Paper Crane*. New York: Greenwillow Books, 1985.

Barrett, Judi. *Animals Should Definitely Not Wear Clothing*. New York: Atheneum, 1970.

Bate, Lucy. *Little Rabbit's Loose Tooth*. New York: Greenwillow Books, 1985.

———. *Little Rabbit's Loose Tooth*. New York: Crown, 1975.

Baylor, Byrd. *I'm in Charge of Celebrations*. New York: Charles Scribner's Sons, 1986.

Blume, Judy. *The Pain and the Great One*. New York: Bradbury Press, 1984.

Bunting, Eve. *The Wednesday Surprise*. New York: Clarion Books, 1989.

Burningham, John. *Hey! Get off Our Train*. New York: Crown, 1989.

Bush, John, and Korky Paul. *The Fish Who Could Wish*. Brooklyn, NY: Kane/Miller, 1991.

Carrick, Carol. *Sleep Out*. New York: Clarion Books, 1973.

Clement, Claude. *The Painter and the Wild Swans*. New York: Dial Press, 1986.

Cohen, Miriam. *Will I Have a Friend?* New York: Macmillan, 1987.

———. *See You in Second Grade*. New York: Greenwillow Books, 1989.

Cooney, Barbara. *Miss Rumphius*. New York: Penguin Books, 1982.

Coville, Bruce, and Katherine Coville. *Sarah's Unicorn*. New York: Lippincott, 1979.

Crowe, Robert L. *Tyler Toad and the Thunder*. New York: Dutton, 1980.

Dayrell, Elphinstone. *Why the Sun and the Moon Live in the Sky*. Boston: Houghton Mifflin, 1968.

dePaola, Tomie. *Strega Nona*. New York: Prentice Hall Press, 1975.

Duvoisin, Roger. *Petunia*. New York: Knopf, 1950.

Fife, Dale H. *The Empty Lot*. Boston: Little, Brown, 1991.

Flora, James. *The Great Green Turkey Creek Monster*. New York: Atheneum, 1976.

Fowles, John. *Cinderella*. Boston: Little, Brown, 1976.

Fox, Mem. *Koala Lou*. San Diego, CA: Harcourt Brace Jovanovich, 1989.

Galdone, Paul. *The Three Billy Goats Gruff*. New York: Clarion Books, 1973.

Geringer, Laura. *A Three Hat Day*. New York: Harper & Row, 1985.

Gibbons, Gail. *Department Store*. New York: Crowell, 1984.

Goble, Paul. *Death of the Iron Horse*. New York: Bradbury Press, 1987.

Grifalconi, Ann. *The Village of Round and Square Houses*. Boston: Little, Brown, 1986.

Hall, Donald. *Ox-Cart Man*. New York: Viking, 1979.

Henkes, Kevin. *Julius, the Baby of the World*. New York: Greenwillow Books, 1990.

Hest, Amy. *The Purple Coat*. New York: Four Winds, 1986.

Hewett, Joan. *Rosalie*. New York: Lothrop, Lee & Shepard, 1987.

Hines, Anna Grossnickle. *Grandma Gets Grumpy*. New York: Clarion Books, 1988.

——. *Sky All Around*. New York: Clarion Books, 1989.

Hort, Lenny. *How Many Stars in the Sky?* New York: Tambourine Books, 1991.

Houston, Gloria. *The Year of the Perfect Christmas Tree: An Appalachian Story*. New York: Dial Press, 1988.

Jeschke, Susan. *Perfect the Pig*. New York: Holt, Rinehart & Winston, 1981.

Jonas, Ann. *Round Trip*. New York: Greenwillow Books, 1983.

Kellogg, Steven. *The Island of the Skog*. New York: Dial Press, 1973.

——. *A Rose for Pinkerton*. New York: Dial Press, 1981.

——. *Pecos Bill*. New York: Morrow, 1986.

Levy, Elizabeth. *Nice Little Girls*. New York: Delacorte, 1978.

Lewin, Hugh. *Jafta*. Minneapolis, MN: Carolrhoda, 1983.

Lionni, Leo. *Alexander and the Wind-up Mouse*. New York: Pantheon Books, 1969.

——. *Matthew's Dream*. New York: Knopf, 1991.

Lobel, Arnold. *Frog and Toad Together*. New York: Harper & Row, 1971.

——. *Mouse Soup*. New York: Harper & Row, 1977.

——. *On Market Street*. New York: Greenwillow Books, 1981.

Locker, Thomas. *The Mare on the Hill*. New York: Dial Press, 1985.

MacLachlan, Patricia. *Through Grandpa's Eyes*. New York: Harper & Row, 1980.

Martin, Bill, Jr., and John Archambault. *Barn Dance!* New York: Henry Holt, 1986.

Mazer, Anne. *The Salamander Room*. New York: Knopf, 1991.

McGovern, Ann. *Stone Soup*. New York: Scholastic, 1986.

McKissack, Patricia. *Mirandy and Brother Wind*. New York: Knopf, 1988.

Miller, Alice. *Mousekin's Fables*. New York: Prentice Hall Press, 1982.

Monjo, F. N. *The Drinking Gourd*. New York: Harper & Row, 1970.

Numeroff, Laura Joffe. *If You Give a Mouse a Cookie*. New York: Harper & Row, 1985.

Ormondroyd, Edward. *Broderick*. Boston: Houghton Mifflin, 1984.

Parish, Peggy. *Amelia Bedelia*. New York: Harper & Row, 1963.

———. *Amelia Bedilia's Family Album*. New York: Greenwillow Books, 1988.

Patterson, Francine. *Koko's Kitten*. New York: Scholastic, 1985.

Peet, Bill. *Big Bad Bruce*. Boston: Houghton Mifflin, 1977.

Pinkwater, Daniel Manus. *The Big Orange Splot*. New York: Scholastic, 1981.

Plume, Ilse. *The Breman Town Musicians* (retold from the Brothers Grimm). New York: Doubleday, 1980.

Polacco, Patricia. *Thunder Cake*. New York: Philomel Books, 1990.

Potter, Beatrix. *The Complete Adventures of Peter Rabbit*. New York: Warne, 1987.

———. *Read-Aloud Rhymes for the Very Young*. New York: Knopf, 1986.

Prelutsky, Jack. *The Baby Uggs Are Hatching*. New York: Greenwillow Books, 1982.

Rylant, Cynthia. *Night in the Country*. New York: Bradbury Press, 1986.

———. *The Relatives Came*. New York: Bradbury Press, 1985.

Schwartz, Amy. *Bea and Mr. Jones*. New York: Bradbury Press, 1982.

Schwartz, David. *How Much Is a Million?* New York: Lothrop, Lee & Shepard, 1985.

Sharmot, Marjorie. *A Big Fat Enormous Lie*. New York: Dutton, 1978.

Shute, Linda. *Momotaro, the Peach Boy*. New York: Lothrop, Lee & Shepard, 1986.

Silverstein, Shel. *The Giving Tree*. New York: Harper & Row, 1964.

Snyder, Dianne. *The Boy of the Three-Year Nap*. Boston: Houghton Mifflin, 1988.

Steig, William. *Amos and Boris*. New York: Farrar, Straus & Giroux, 1971.

Steiner, Barbara. *The Whale Brother*. New York: Walker, 1988.

Stevenson, James. *Will You Please Feed Our Cat?* New York: Greenwillow Books, 1987.

Turkle, Brinton. *Thy Friend, Obadiah*. New York: Viking, 1969.

Van Allsburg, Chris. *Jumanji*. Boston: Houghton Mifflin, 1981.

———. *Two Bad Ants*. Boston: Houghton Mifflin, 1988.

Viorst, Judith. *Alexander, Who Used to Be Rich Last Sunday*. New York: Atheneum, 1978.

———. *I'll Fix Anthony*. New York: Harper & Row, 1969.

Waber, Bernard. *An Anteater Named Arthur*. Boston: Houghton Mifflin, 1967.

———. *Lovable Lyle*. Boston: Houghton Mifflin, 1969.

Wadsworth, Olive. *Over in the Meadow: A Counting-Out Rhyme*. New York: Viking, 1985.

Weiss, Nicki. *Princess Pearl*. New York: Greenwillow Books, 1986.

Yolen, Jane. *Owl Moon*. New York: Philomel Books, 1987.

Yorinks, Arthur. *Hey, Al*. New York: Farrar, Straus & Giroux, 1986.

Zelinsky, Paul. *Rumpelstiltskin* (retold from the Brothers Grimm). New York: Dutton, 1986.

Zemach, Margot. *It Could Always Be Worse*. New York: Farrar, Straus & Giroux, 1976.

Grades 3–4

Aardema, Verna. *Traveling to Tondo*. New York: Knopf, 1991.

Asch, Frank. *Pearl's Promise*. New York: Delacorte, 1984.

Babbitt, Natalie. *The Search for Delicious*. New York: Farrar, Straus & Giroux, 1969.

Baum, L. Frank. *The (Wonderful) Wizard of Oz*. New York: Holt, 1983.

Blume, Judy. *The One in the Middle Is the Green Kangaroo*. New York: Dell, 1981.

———. *Tales of a Fourth Grade Nothing*. New York: Dutton, 1972.

Brett, Jan. *Berlioz the Bear*. New York: Putnam, 1991.

Bulla, Clyde. *The Chalk Box Kid*. New York: Random House, 1987.

———. *The Shoeshine Girl*. New York: Crowell, 1975.

Burch, Robert. *Ida Early Comes over the Mountain*. New York: Viking, 1980.

Burnett, Frances Hodgson. *Sara Crewe*. New York: Putnam, 1981.

Byars, Betsy. *Trouble River*. New York: Viking, 1969.

Carrick, Carol. *Sleep Out*. New York: Clarion Books, 1973.

Carrick, Carol, and Donald Carrick. *Old Mother Witch*. New York: Clarion Books, 1975.

Catling, Patrick S. *The Chocolate Touch*. New York: Morrow, 1979.

Chew, Ruth. *No Such Thing As a Witch*. New York: Hastings House, 1971.

Cleary, Beverly. *Dear Mr. Henshaw*. New York: Morrow, 1983.

———. *Ramona Forever*. New York: Morrow, 1984.

———. *Ramona the Brave*. New York: Morrow, 1975.

Clifford, Eth. *Help! I'm a Prisoner in the Library*. Boston: Houghton Mifflin, 1979.

Clifton, Lucille. *The Lucky Stone*. New York: Delacorte, 1979.

Cole, Joanna. *The Magic School Bus at the Waterworks*. New York: Scholastic, 1986.

Cone, Molly. *Mishmash and the Big Fat Problem*. New York: Archway, 1982.

Cooney, Barbara. *Hattie and the Wild Waves*. New York: Viking, 1990.

Corcoran, Barbara. *The Long Journey*. New York: Atheneum, 1970.

Coville, Bruce. *The Monster's Ring*. New York: Pantheon Books, 1982.

Dahl, Roald. *Danny the Champion of the World*. New York: Knopf, 1978.

———. *James and the Giant Peach*. New York: Knopf, 1961.

Davis, Deborah. *The Secret of the Seal*. New York: Crown, 1989.

dePaola, Tomie. *The Legend of the Indian Paintbrush*. New York: Putnam, 1988.

Donnelly, Judy. *The Titanic Lost and Found*. New York: Random House, 1987.

Erickson, Russell. *Warton and Morton*. New York: Morrow, 1976.

Farley, Walter. *The Black Stallion*. New York: Random House, 1944.

Fleischman, Paul. *The Half-a-Moon Inn*. New York: Harper & Row, 1980.

Fowles, John. *Cinderella*. Boston: Little, Brown, 1976.

Fredericks, Anthony D. *Clever Camouflagers*. Minocqua, WI: NorthWord Press, 1997.

———. *Weird Walkers*. Minocqua, WI: NorthWord Press, 1996.

Green, Phyllis. *Wild Violets*. New York: Dell, 1980.

Greenfield, Eloise. *Nathaniel Talking*. New York: Black Butterfly Children's Books, 1988.

Greenwald, Sheila. *Rosy Cole's Great American Guilt Club*. New York: Atlantic Monthly, 1985.

Grifalconi, Ann. *The Village of Round and Square Houses*. Boston: Little, Brown, 1986.

Gwynne, Fred. *The King Who Rained*. New York: Simon & Schuster, 1970.

Haas, Irene. *The Maggie B*. New York: Atheneum, 1975.

Harding, Lee. *The Fallen Spaceman*. New York: Bantam, 1982.

Heide, Florence Parry. *The Shrinking of Treehorn*. New York: Holiday House, 1971.

Himmelman, John. *Ibis: A True Whale Story*. New York: Scholastic, 1990.

Holland, Barbara. *Prisoners at the Kitchen Table*. New York: Clarion Books, 1979.

Hurwitz, Johanna. *Class Clown*. New York: Morrow, 1987.

———. *Much Ado About Aldo*. New York: Morrow, 1978.

Kaye, M. M. *The Ordinary Princess*. New York: Doubleday, 1984.

Kennedy, Richard. *Inside My Feet: The Story of a Giant*. New York: Harper & Row, 1979.

Kessler, Leonard. *Old Turtle's Ninety Knock-Knocks, Jokes, & Riddles*. New York: Greenwillow Books, 1991.

Kline, Suzy. *Orp*. New York: Putnam, 1989.

Lang, Andrew. *Aladdin*. New York: Puffin, 1983.

Levoy, Myron. *The Witch of Fourth Street*. New York: Harper & Row, 1972.

Levy, Elizabeth. *Frankenstein Moved in on the Fourth Floor*. New York: Harper & Row, 1979.

———. *Something Queer Is Going On*. New York: Dell, 1973.

Lewis, C. S. *The Lion, the Witch and the Wardrobe*. New York: Macmillan, 1950.

Lord, Bette Bao. *In the Year of the Boar and Jackie Robinson*. New York: Harper & Row, 1984.

Maclachlan, Patricia. *Through Grandpa's Eyes*. New York: Harper & Row, 1980.

Manes, Stephen. *Be a Perfect Person in Just Three Days*. New York: Clarion Books, 1982.

Mayer, Mercer. *East of the Sun and West of the Moon*. New York: Four Winds, 1980.

Mazer, Norma Fox. *Mrs. Fish, Ape, and Me, the Dump Queen*. New York: Dutton, 1980.

Miles, Bernard. *Robin Hood—Prince of Outlaws*. New York: Rand McNally, 1979.

Monjo, F. N. *The Drinking Gourd*. New York: Harper and Row, 1970.

Mowat, Farley. *Owls in the Family*. Boston: Little, Brown, 1961.

Nichols, Ruth. *A Walk out of the World*. New York: Harcourt, Brace & World, 1969.

O'Dell, Scott. *Sing Down the Moon*. Boston: Houghton Mifflin, 1970.

Parker, Nancy Winslow, and Joan Richards Wright. *Frogs, Toads, Lizards, and Salamanders*. New York: Greenwillow Books, 1990.

Peet, Bill. *The Wingdingdilly*. Boston: Houghton Mifflin, 1970.

Peterson, John. *The Littles*. New York: Scholastic, 1970.

Prelutsky, Jack. *The New Kid on the Block*. New York: Greenwillow Books, 1984.

———. *Nightmares: Poems to Trouble Your Sleep*. New York: Greenwillow Books, 1976.

Rawls, Wilson. *Where the Red Fern Grows*. New York: Doubleday, 1961.

Richler, Mordecai. *Jacob Two-Two Meets the Hooded Fang*. New York: Knopf, 1975.

Robinson, Barbara. *The Best Christmas Pageant Ever*. New York: Harper & Row, 1972.

Seldon, George. *Cricket in Times Square*. New York: Farrar, Straus & Giroux, 1960.

Shreve, Susan. *Family Secrets: Five Very Important Stories*. New York: Knopf, 1979.

Silverstein, Shel. *The Giving Tree*. New York: Harper & Row, 1964.

———. *Lafcadio, the Lion Who Shot Back*. New York: Harper & Row, 1963.

———. *Where the Sidewalk Ends*. New York: Harper & Row, 1974.

Slater, Jim. *Grasshopper and the Unwise Owl*. New York: Henry Holt, 1979.

Smith, Robert K. *Chocolate Fever*. New York: Dell, 1978.

Sobol, Donald. *Encyclopedia Brown and the Case of the Midnight Visitor*. New York: Lodestar, 1977.

Speare, Elizabeth George. *The Sign of the Beaver*. Boston: Houghton Mifflin, 1983.

Stearns, Pamela. *Into the Painted Bear Lair*. Boston: Houghton Mifflin, 1976.

Steig, William. *The Real Thief*. New York: Farrar, Straus & Giroux, 1973.

———. *Sylvester and the Magic Pebble*. New York: Simon & Schuster, 1969.

Thiele, Colin. *Storm Boy*. New York: Harper & Row, 1978.

Thomas, Jane Resh. *The Comeback Dog*. New York: Clarion Books, 1981.

van der Meer, Ron, and Atie van der Meer. *Amazing Animal Senses*. Boston: Little, Brown, 1990.

Viorst, Judith. *If I Were in Charge of the World and Other Worries*. New York: Atheneum, 1981.

Wagner, Jane. *J.T.* New York: Dell, 1971.

Wallace, Bill. *A Dog Called Kitty*. New York: Holiday House, 1980.

Weller, Frances Ward. *Riptide*. New York: Philomel Books, 1990.

White, E. B. *Charlotte's Web*. New York: Harper & Row, 1952.

Williams, Margery. *The Velveteen Rabbit*. New York: Knopf, 1985.

Willis, Val. *The Secret in the Matchbox*. New York: Farrar, Straus & Giroux, 1988.

Wolitzer, Hilma. *Introducing Shirley Braverman*. New York: Farrar, Straus & Giroux, 1975.

Grades 5–6

Alexander, Lloyd. *Westmark*. New York: Dutton, 1981.

Avi. *Captain Grey*. New York: Pantheon Books, 1977.

———. *Emily Upham's Revenge*. New York: Pantheon Books, 1978.

Babbitt, Natalie. *Tuck Everlasting*. New York: Farrar, Straus & Giroux, 1975.

Baker, Olaf. *Where the Buffaloes Begin*. New York: Warne, 1981.

Banks, Lynne Reid. *The Indian in the Cupboard*. New York: Doubleday, 1981.

Baylor, Byrd. *Hawk, I'm Your Brother*. New York: Charles Scribner's Sons, 1976.

Beatty, Patricia. *Lupita Manana*. New York: Morrow, 1981.

Bethancourt, T. Ernesto. *The Dog Days of Arthur Cane*. New York: Holiday House, 1976.

Blos, Joan W. *A Gathering of Days: A New England Girl's Journal, 1830–32*. New York: Scribner's, 1979.

Blue, Rose. *Grandma Didn't Wave Back*. New York: Watts, 1972.

Blume, Judy. *Are You There God? It's Me, Margaret*. New York: Bradbury Press, 1970.

———. *Then Again, Maybe I Won't*. New York: Bradbury Press, 1971.

———. *Otherwise Known As Sheila the Great*. New York: Dutton, 1972.

Brink, Carol R. *The Bad Times of Irma Baumlein*. New York: Macmillan, 1972.

———. *Caddie Woodlawn*. New York: Macmillan, 1973.

Brittain, Bill. *The Wish Giver*. New York: Harper & Row, 1983.

Byars, Betsy. *The Cybil War*. New York: Viking, 1981.

———. *The 18th Emergency*. New York: Viking, 1973.

———. *Good-Bye, Chicken Little*. New York: Harper & Row, 1979.

———. *The Midnight Fox*. New York: Viking, 1978.

Callen, Larry. *Pinch*. Boston: Little, Brown, 1976.

Cleary, Beverly. *Ramona the Brave*. New York: Morrow, 1975.

Cleaver, Vera, and Bill Cleaver. *Queen of Hearts*. New York: Lippincott, 1978.

———. *Where the Lilies Bloom*. New York: Lippincott, 1969.

Cohen, Barbara. *R, My Name Is Rosie*. New York: Lothrop, Lee & Shepard, 1978.

———. *Thank You, Jackie Robinson*. New York: Lothrop, Lee & Shepard, 1974.

Collier, James L., and Christopher Collier. *Jump Ship to Freedom*. New York: Delacorte, 1982.

———. *My Brother Sam Is Dead*. New York: Four Winds, 1974.

Cormier, Robert. *The Chocolate War*. New York: Dell, 1986.

Cunningham, Julia. *Burnish Me Bright*. New York: Dell, 1980.

Dahl, Roald. *Danny the Champion of the World*. New York: Knopf, 1978.

———. *The Wonderful Story of Henry Sugar and Six More*. New York: Knopf, 1977.

Duncan, Lois. *Killing Mr. Griffin*. Boston: Little, Brown, 1978.

Estes, Eleanor. *The Hundred Dresses*. New York: Harcourt Brace Jovanovich, 1974.

Farley, Walter. *The Black Stallion*. New York: Random House, 1944.

Fleischman, Paul. *Path of the Pale Horse*. New York: Harper & Row, 1983.

Fox, Paula. *One-Eyed Cat*. New York: Bradbury Press, 1984.

———. *Slave Dancer*. New York: Bradbury Press, 1973.

Fredericks, Anthony D. *Exploring the Rainforest*. Golden, CO: Fulcrum, 1996.

———. *Surprising Swimmers*. Minnetonka, MN: NorthWord Press, 1996.

Freedman, Russell. *Lincoln: A Photobiography*. New York: Clarion Books, 1987.

Fritz, Jean. *Where Do You Think You're Going Christopher Columbus?* New York: Putnam, 1980.

George, Jean Craighead. *Julie of the Wolves*. New York: Harper & Row, 1972.

Goble, Paul. *Buffalo Woman*. New York: Bradbury Press, 1984.

———. *Death of the Iron Horse*. New York: Bradbury Press, 1987.

Graeber, Charlotte. *Grey Cloud*. New York: Four Winds, 1979.

Highwater, Jamake. *Journey to the Sky*. New York: Crowell, 1978.

Holm, Anne. *North to Freedom*. New York: Harcourt, Brace & World, 1974.

Holman, Felice. *Slake's Limbo*. New York: Charles Scribner's Sons, 1984.

Hopkins, Lee Bennett. *Mama*. New York: Knopf, 1977.

Hunter, Mollie. *A Stranger Came Ashore*. New York: Harper & Row, 1975.

Konigsburg, E. L. *From the Mixed-Up Files of Mrs. Basil Frankweiler*. New York: Atheneum, 1967.

Lee, Robert C. *It's a Mile from Here to Glory*. Boston: Little, Brown, 1972.

LeGuin, Ursula K. *Catwings*. New York: Watts, 1988.

L'Engle, Madeleine. *A Swiftly Tilting Planet*. New York: Farrar, Straus & Giroux, 1978.

London, Jack. *The Call of the Wild*. New York: Penguin Books, 1981.

Lowry, Lois. *Anastasia Krupnik*. Boston: Houghton Mifflin, 1979.

———. *Number the Stars*. Boston: Houghton Mifflin, 1989.

Magorian, Michelle. *Good Night, Mr. Tom*. New York: Harper & Row, 1981.

Maruki, Toshi. *Hiroshima No Pika*. New York: Lothrop, Lee & Shepard, 1982.

Mayer, Franklyn. *Me and Caleb*. New York: Scholastic, 1982.

Mazer, Harry. *Cave under the City*. New York: Crowell, 1986.

———. *Snow-Bound*. New York: Delacorte, 1973.

Mazer, Norma Fox. *After the Rain*. New York: Morrow, 1987.

McKissack, Patricia. *Mirandy and Brother Wind*. New York: Knopf, 1988.

Mowat, Farley. *Owls in the Family*. Boston: Little, Brown, 1961.

Murphy, Jim. *Death Run*. New York: Clarion Books, 1982.

Myers, Walter Dean. *Scorpions*. New York: Harper & Row, 1988.

Newman, Robert. *The Case of the Baker Street Irregular*. New York: Atheneum, 1978.

O'Dell, Scott. *Sarah Bishop*. New York: Houghton Mifflin, 1980.

———. *Sing Down the Moon*. Boston: Houghton Mifflin, 1970.

Paterson, Katherine. *The Great Gilly Hopkins*. New York: Crowell, 1978.

Paulsen, Gary. *Hatchet*. New York: Bradbury Press, 1987.

Peck, Robert. *A Day No Pigs Would Die*. New York: Knopf, 1972.

Raskin, Ellen. *The Westing Game*. New York: Dutton, 1978.

Rodgers, Mary. *Freaky Friday*. New York: Harper & Row, 1972.

Salassi, Otto. *And Nobody Knew They Were There*. New York: Greenwillow Books, 1984.

Sargent, Sarah. *Weird Henry Berg*. New York: Crown, 1980.

Schwartz, Alvin. *Scary Stories to Tell in the Dark*. New York: Harper & Row, 1983.

Sebestyen, Ouida. *Words by Heart*. New York: Bantam, 1981.

Seidler, Tor. *Terpin*. New York: Farrar, Straus & Giroux, 1982.

Shreve, Susan. *Family Secrets: Five Very Important Stories*. New York: Knopf, 1979.

Silverstein, Shel. *A Light in the Attic*. New York: Harper & Row, 1981.

Singer, Isaac B. *Zlateh the Goat and Other Stories*. New York: Harper & Row, 1966.

Sleator, William. *Among the Dolls*. New York: Dutton, 1975.

Slote, Alfred. *Hang Tough, Paul Mather*. New York: Lippincott, 1973.

———. *The Trading Game*. New York: Lippincott, 1990.

Smith, Doris. *A Taste of Blackberries*. New York: Crowell, 1973.

Speare, Elizabeth George. *The Sign of the Beaver*. Boston: Houghton Mifflin, 1983.

Sperry, Armstrong. *Call It Courage*. New York: Macmillan, 1971.

Stoltz, Mary. *Cider Days*. New York: Harper & Row, 1978.

Taylor, Mildred. *Roll of Thunder, Hear My Cry*. New York: Dial Press, 1976.

Taylor, Theodore. *The Cay*. New York: Doubleday, 1969.

Uchida, Yoshiko. *Journey to Topaz*. New York: Charles Scribner's, 1971.

Voigt, Cynthia. *Dicey's Song*. New York: Atheneum, 1982.

Wallace, Barbara. *Peppermints in the Parlor*. New York: Atheneum, 1980.

Yep, Lawrence. *Child of the Owl*. New York: Harper & Row, 1977.

———. *Dragonwings*. New York: Harper & Row, 1975.

WEB SITES

The following Web sites can provide you with valuable background information, a wealth of literature resources, scores of up-to-date lesson plans, and numerous tools for expanding any area of your language arts curriculum. They can become important adjuncts to any literature-based reading program and can be used by teachers and students alike.

[NOTE: These Web sites were current and accurate as of the writing of this book. Please be aware that some may change, others may be eliminated, and new ones will be added to the various search engines that you use at home or at school.]

http://www.afredericks.com

This Web site is designed to provide busy classroom teachers with the latest information, the newest activities, and some of the most creative ideas for using children's literature across the curriculum—with a special emphasis on the science curriculum. It's updated frequently with hundreds of exciting projects.

http://www.acs.ucalgary.ca/~dkbrown

This is the ultimate compendium of literature resources. It includes book awards, authors on the Web, book reviews, recommended books, book discussion groups, children's literature organizations, best sellers, and scores of teaching ideas.

http://www.carolhurst.com/

This site has a wonderful collection of reviews of great books for kids, ideas of ways to use them in the classroom, and collections of books and activities about particular subjects, curricular areas, themes, and professional topics.

http://www.scils.rutgers.edu/special/kay/childlit.html

Here you'll find lots of resources and valuable information on how to effectively use children's literature in the classroom. The focus is on multiple genres and various methods for promoting good books to all ages and all abilities.

http://www.users.interport.net/~fairrosa

Here are articles, reviews, lists, links, authors, discussions, and monthly updates about the best in children's literature and how to share it with kids. This is a great site for the always busy classroom teacher.

http://www.ipl.org

This is the Internet Public Library—an overwhelming assembly of collections and resources of a large public library. This site covers just about every topic in children's literature with an incredible array of resources.

http://www.ccn.cs.dal.ca/~aa331/childlit.html#review

This site is dedicated to reviewing WWW resources related to children's literature and youth services. These resources are aimed towards school librarians, children's writers, illustrators, book reviewers, storytellers, parents, and teachers.

http://i-site.on.ca/booknook.html

This site is a repository of book reviews for kids written by other kids. The reviews are categorized by grade level: K–3, 4–6, 7–9, and 10–12. It's a great way to find out what's popular among young readers.

http://www.armory.com/~web/notes.html

This site provides reviews of children's literature written by teachers and others who love kids' books. It's an electronic journal of book reviews concentrating on how well books are written and how well they entertain.

Index

A Is for Africa, 85
Aardema, Verna, 110
Ability grouping, 5
Achievement, academic, 2
Adjectives list, 128
Advertising
    for animal favorite, 48
    by book characters, 162
    about books, 9, 10, 119
    classified, 12, 155
    environmental, 107
Africa, 20–21, 85, 87, 109–12
Africa (video), 85
African Odyssey (video), 85
African Wildlife (video), 85
Africa's Stolen River (video), 85
Air, Light, and Water, 159
Alexander and the Terrible, Horrible, No Good, Very Bad Day, 66–68
Aliens Ate My Homework, 141
Aliki, 159
Allard, Harry, 90
Allen, Linda, 151
Alligators, 63
Alphabet, and reptiles, 63
American Indian as Farmer, The, 159
American Indians: A Brief History (video), 160
America's Fascinating Indian Heritage, 158, 159
Analogies, sharing, 19
Animals. *See also* Living things
    adoption of, 108
    African, 110
    baby, 47, 75, 77, 134
    in commercials, 45
    homes of, 137
    observation of, 94
    in product names, 58
    sounds of, 65, 76, 79, 136
    study of, 46–49
    tracks of, 48
    unusual, 117–20
Animals at the Water's Edge, 33
Animals on the Farm (video), 127
Ant Cities, 41
Anticipation guides, 24–26
Antonyms, 28, 32
Ants, 40
Apple Tree Christmas, 77
Aquariums, 42–43, 61, 85
Arnold, Caroline, 20

Art. *See also* Collages; Illustrations
    book covers, 10, 86
    in bookweb, 36fig, 37
    cards, 85, 162
    castle/palace, 67, 104
    caterpillars, 61
    corn necklace, 148
    milk pictures, 75
    murals, 70
    Native American, 159
    paintings, study of, 14, 148
    shelter montage, 13
    snake replica, 78
Artifacts, display of, 14, 44, 51
Asbjørnsen, P. C., 103
Ashanti to Zulu, 85
Assignments, self correcting, 5
At the Frog Pond, 156
Auctions, 9, 14
Audiotapes, student, 11, 19, 46, 66, 102, 136
Australia, 66–68
Authors, 5, 9, 10, 11, 138, 139

Backyard Bird Watching, 85
Baker, Olaf, 158
Baldwin, Gordon, 159
Barrett, Judi, 97
Bartering system, 160
Barton, Byron, 66, 81
Bathwater Gang, The, 69–71
Bean Soup, recipe for, 51–52
Bears, 57–59, 89
Bears (Penny), 58
Bears (Petty), 58
Bears for Kids, 58
Bears on Hemlock Mountain, 147
Bender, Lionel, 66
Bernheim, Evelyne, 111
Bernheim, Marc, 85, 111
Biographies, 107, 146
Birds, 47, 85, 143
Black and White Salad, recipe for, 153
Blood and Guts: A Working Guide to Your Own Insides, 151
Blume, Judy, 155
Body Atlas, The, 151
Bond, Jean, 85
Bones, Bones, Dinosaur Bones, 81
Bonne, Rose, 46

Book creation, 9
   butterfly books, 37, 60
   cookbook, 11
   dragon books, 142
   flip books, 14, 129
   picture books, 12, 126–27
   pop-up book, 14
Book extension activities, 8–15
Book reviews, Web sites for, 178
Bookwebbing techniques, 36–38
Borden, Beatrice, 85
Box Turtle at Long Pond, 156
Brainstorming, 26, 28, 36, 40, 47
Brazil, 108
Brin, Ruth, 61
Brinckloe, J., 40
Buffalo, 159, 160
Bugs, 39–42
Bunting, Eve, 131
Burnie, David, 114
Burns, Diane, 63
Bushmen of the Kalihari (video), 85
Butterflies, 60–62, 139
Butterflies Are Beautiful, 61

Canfield, Jane White, 103
Carle, Eric, 60
Cassidy, Nancy, 112
Categorization
   of animals, 47, 78, 104
   of books, 3
   of information, 22, 23
   of words, 20–21
Caterpillars, 60–62
Cats, 145
Caught in the Moving Mountains, 147
Cauley, Lorinda Bryan, 50
Cay, The, 147
Cerf, Bennett, 144
Chalktalk, 14
Character Continuum, 28–31
Charts/graphs
   bear life span, 58
   book data, 11, 13
   literary activities, 132
   longevity, 76
   nutritional needs, 162
   plants/trees, 51, 95, 107
   population, 41, 79, 136
   size measures, 12, 48, 56, 82, 143, 162
   sleep habits, 89
   survey results, 104
   toad/frog data, 43–44
   travel speed, 61, 64, 79
   weather, 13, 99–100

Cherry, Lynne, 106
Children's Crafts, 111
Choices, opportunities for, 3, 8
Classroom environment, 6, 91, 95, 107
Clay, homemade, recipe for, 104
Cleary, Beverly, 37, 138
Clever Camouflagers, 134–37
Climate logbook, 13
Cloudy with a Chance of Meatballs, 97–101
Clubs, 9, 108
Coerr, Eleanor, 151
Collages
   animal, 89, 107, 126, 162
   artifacts, 51
   book events, 11
   family, 132
   haunted house, 145
   insects, 40
   trucks, 37, 139
Collard, Sneed, 114
Comic strips, 11, 51
Comprehension
   participatory, 16–34
   and prediction cards, 20, 21
   self assessment of, 5, 19
   strategic, 35
Constellations, 59
Corn Is Maize: The Gift of the Indians, 159
Cosgrove, Brian, 159
Cosner, Sharon, 81
Costumes, 10, 111, 112, 163
Coville, Bruce, 141
Cow, 72–76
Cows, 72–76
Creativity, 2
Creepy Crawly Caterpillars, 61
Crocker, Mark, 151
Curriculum, integrated, 6, 7–15, 26, 35–38

Dalgleish, Alice, 147
Dance, Art and Ritual of Africa, The, 112
Dance of Africa: An Introduction, The, 112
Day Jimmy's Boa Ate the Wash, The, 77–79
Dayrell, Elphinstone, 30
Days with Frog and Toad, 42
Dear Mr. Henshaw, 37, 138–40
Deep in the Forest, 147
Dental care, 155
Developmental stages, 56
DeWitt, Linda, 97
Diaries
   book impressions in, 11
   life events in, 148
   other viewpoints in, 49, 63, 78, 84
   and seasonal changes, 114

Dictionaries, 12, 110, 142
Dinosaur Dinners, 81
Dinosaurs, 63, 80–83
Dinosaurs (Hopkins), 81
Dinosaurs (Wexo), 81
Dinosaurs: Strange and Wonderful, 80–83
Dioramas, 14, 86, 143
Discovering Dinosaur Babies, 81
Dorros, Arthur, 41
Dragons, 141–43
Drama
    and book content, 10, 14, 58, 69
    in bookweb, 36fig, 37
    mime/pantomime, 14, 96
    play writing, 11, 37
    radio shows, 14, 154
    role playing, 10, 14, 15, 96
    and voice inflection, 69–70

Earthquakes, 128, 129
Earthquakes and Volcanoes (video), 128
Earthworks Group, 108
East of the Sun and West of the Moon
    (Hague), 103
East of the Sun and West of the Moon
    (Mayer), 102–5
East of the Sun and West of the Moon:
    A Play (Willard), 103
Easy Origami, 153
Eckert, Allan W., 147
Ecology, 13, 25, 26, 108
England, 163
Evaluation
    of books, 3, 4, 9, 11, 14, 15
    of lesson materials, 4–5
    self assessment, 4–5, 19
Everyday Things and How They Work, 67
Expectations, 6, 16

Facklam, Margery, 61
Facts/Attitude Continuum, 32–33
Fair, Jeff, 58
Faithful Elephants, The, 151
Family Songbook, 71
Famous Ghost Stories, 144
Feelings, Muriel, 85
Field trips, 64, 100, 106, 137, 152
Fifty Things Kids Can Do to Save the Earth,
    108
Fins, Feathers, Fur: Animal Groups (film), 47
Fireflies, 40
Fish, age of, 119–20
Fleischman, Sid, 161

Florian, Douglas, 156
Flour dough, recipe for, 55
Flower children, 69
Flunking of Joshua T. Bates, The, 84–87
Folktales
    African, 110
    bears in, 59
    dragons in, 143
    fractured, 72–74, 121–26
    and mock trials, 53
    scary stories, 146
    as tradition, 52, 102, 163
    and volcanoes, 128
Force: The Power Behind Movement, 67
Forests, 114
Fox, Dan, editor, 71, 105
Frantic Frogs and Other Frankly Fractured
    Folktales for Readers Theatre, 121
Fredericks, Anthony D., 63, 72, 117, 121, 134
Friendship, 42, 84
Frog and Toad All Year, 42
Frog and Toad Are Friends, 42–45
Frog and Toad Pop Up Book, The, 42
Frog Prince, The, 103
Frogs/toads, 42–45, 61, 102–3
Fudge, recipe for, 156–57

Gackenbach, Dick, 114
Galdone, Paul, 57
Gamlin, Linda, 114
Ganeri, Anita, 159
Gangs, 69–71
George, Jean Craighead, 147
George, William, 156
Giant Bears of Kodiak Island (video), 58
Gibbons, Gail, 24, 97
Girl from Yamhill, A, 138
Go in and out the Window, 105
Goal setting, 2, 4
Golden Book of Insects and Spiders, The, 40
Grandparents, 11, 69, 87, 131, 163
Gray, Alice, 153
Great Crystal Bear, 58
Great Kapok Tree, The, 106–8
Green Giants, 114
Greer, Allen, 63
Grizzlies, The (video), 58

Hague, Kathleen, 103
Hague, Michael, 103
Hansy's Mermaid, 77
Harbin, Robert, 153
Harrison, George H., 85

Haunted England: A Survey of English Ghostlore, 146
Health, in bookweb, 36fig, 37
Healthcare, 75, 85, 152, 155
Henry and Beezus, 138
Hippo, 20
History, 12, 13, 37, 139–40, 146, 163
Hofsinde, Robert, 159
Hole, Christina, 146
Holidays, 133
Hornblow, A., 40
Hornblow, L., 40
How Did Dinosaurs Live?, 81
Huet, Michael, 112
Hughes, Langston, 112
Human body
    books about, 151
    digestive system, 72, 126
    excretory system, 126
    muscle system, 152, 154
    outline drawing of, 54
    sensory system, 162
    skeletal system, 145, 152, 154
Human Body and How It Works, The, 151

I Know an Old Lady, 46–49
I Left My Sneakers in Dimension X, 141
Identification cards, 58
Illustrations
    of animals, 47, 48, 95
    based on book, 11, 14, 43, 48,
        143, 145
    of book characters, 14
    comparison of, 82, 95, 114
    creation of, 13, 37, 119
    importance of, 95
    of insects, 40
    and SMART questions, 17
    and volcanoes, 129
In Africa, 85, 111
Incident at Hawk's Hill, 147
Incredible Human Machine, The
    (video), 152
Independence, student, 4, 9
Indian and the Buffalo, The, 159
Indians of the Northern Plains, 159
Indians of the Southern Plains, 159
Indians of the Southwest, 159
Insectasides, 46
Insects, 39–41, 46
Insects Do the Strangest Things, 40
Insects That Live in Families, 40
Integrated curriculum, 6, 7–15, 26
Interest inventories, 3

Interviews
    with experts, 12, 81, 85, 94, 157
    family, 66, 131, 133, 154, 163
    in neighborhood, 10, 66, 87
    with students, 69
Invention, 66
Invisible World, The (video), 152
Ira Sleeps Over, 88–89

Jack and the Beanstalk, 50–53
Jambo Means Hello, 85
Janvier, Thomas, 146
Japan, 151, 153–54
Jenkins, Ella, 112
Jennifer Murdley's Toad, 141
Jeremy Thatcher, Dragon Hatcher,
    141–43
Jones, Louis, 144
Joslin, Sesyle, 157
Journals
    of animal sightings, 47, 79, 135
    book impressions in, 11
    field observation, 49, 94, 135
    plant/tree growth in, 54, 106
    and seasonal changes, 114
    for tutoring bureau, 84
Journey to the Forgotten River (video), 85
Julivert, Angel, 40
Junk food, 75

Kidsongs, 112
King's Tea, The, 77
Knowledge, background, 20, 21, 22,
    24, 27, 32
Kraus, Robert, 54
Kunihiko, Hisa, 81
K-W-L (What I Know, Want to Learn,
    Learned), 22–23

Laithwaite, Eric, 67
Lambert, David, 114
Language arts, 7, 9, 26
    in bookweb, 36fig, 38
    skills, 6
Lavies, Bianca, 156
Leach, Maria, 144
Leadership skills, 71
Learning styles, 6
Legends of the City of Mexico, 146
Leo the Late Bloomer, 54–56
Leslie, Clare, 97
Lesser, Carolyn, 58

Letter writing
    to authors, 11, 138–39
    from book character, 12, 106
    to book character, 11, 42, 85, 91, 141, 144, 158
    and endangered species, 58
    to friends, 11
    to historical figure, 11
    and nutrition, 75
    pen pals, 15, 38, 70, 87, 139
    to publishers, 40
Life cycles, 58, 60, 100, 162
Life jackets, 18
Life of the American Indian, The (film), 160
Lily Pad Pond, 156
Lions of the African Night (video), 85
Literacy rates, 133
Literature
    in curriculum, 35–38
    in reading program, 5
    supplemental, by grade, 165–76
    Web sites for, 178
Living things. *See also* Animals; Plants
    African, 20, 85, 110
    anticipation guide for, 25–26
    and camouflage, 134–37
    in containers, 40, 42–43, 61, 85, 103
    endangered, 58, 135, 136
    and hibernation, 148
    and life cycles, 162
Lobel, Arnold, 42
Locker, Thomas, 113
Luenn, Nancy, 114

Macauley, David, 67
Machines and How They Work, 67
Machines and Movement, 67
Machines at Work, 66
Magazines, 14, 40, 81, 101, 135, 162
Magic of Origami, The, 153
Make Your Own Dinosaur out of Chicken Bones, 142
Making Musical Things, 105
Man: The Incredible Machine (film), 145
Manners, 157
Maps
    of Africa, 112
    and animal locations, 65, 76, 96, 120, 137
    and climate, 13
    community, 71
    and dinosaurs, 83
    and distance measures, 12, 139
    and dragon histories, 143
    of Japan, 153
    of kingdom, 163

    and rain forests, 108
    salt, 14, 71
    story, 12
    topological, 149
    and travel routes, 112
    treasure, 101
    and weather patterns, 100, 101
Markle, Sandra, 97, 114, 151
Materials, sources of
    container animals, 43, 61, 85, 103
    electronics, 139
    fossils, 81
    music, 86, 95, 107, 120
    nature sounds, 41, 107
    skeleton model, 145
Math. *See also* Charts/graphs; Timelines
    batting averages, 86, 143, 145
    in bookweb, 36fig, 37
    computations, 86, 139–40, 143, 145–46, 160
    distances between places, 12, 139
    measurements, 82, 111, 115, 160
    perfect assignment for, 91
    prices, 100, 160
    recipe adjustments, 51, 76, 127, 149, 153, 157
    reptile data, 64
    temperatures, 99–100, 129
    time zones, 86
    tree rings, 95, 107
    volcanoes, 129
    word problems, 70–71
Mayer, Mercer, 102
Mayo, G., 116
Mazer, Anne, 25, 93
McGowan, Chris, 142
McMillan, Bruce, 97
Meanwhile Back at the Ranch, 77
Michels, Tilde, 156
Mighty Tree, 114
Milne, Charles P., 33
Miss Nelson Has a Field Day, 91
Miss Nelson Is Back, 91
Miss Nelson Is Missing, 90–92
MM & M (Metacognitive Modeling and Monitoring), 18–20
Mock trials, 53
Model creation
    animals, 48, 70, 95
    book characters, 13, 14, 104
    book location, 12
    family members, 132
    hand/foot castings, 55
    historical sites, 13
    houses, 111
    salt maps, 14

Moe, Jørgon E., 103
Money systems, 104, 162
Monster's Ring, The, 141
More Scary Stories to Tell in the Dark, 144–46
Morris, D., 40
Morris, Luverne, 159
Motivation, 1, 2, 6, 16, 35
Mufaro's Beautiful Daughters, 109–12
Mural creation, 70
Museums, 14, 44, 148
Musgrove, Margaret, 85
Music
    African, 86, 112
    animal theme, 127
    associated with characters, 14, 58, 143
    background, 14, 52, 56, 133, 154
    in bookweb, 36fig, 38
    classical, 38, 65, 105, 163
    comparisons of, 149
    environmental, 95
    folksongs, 14, 105, 112, 163
    Japanese, 153
    Native American, 160
    sound effects, 76, 146
    water related, 71, 120
Musical instruments
    African, recorded, 86, 112
    and animals, 62, 65, 163
    making, 105, 112, 163
    and sound effects, 76
    wooden, 116
My Side of the Mountain, 147–50
My Teacher Flunked the Planet, 141
My Teacher Fried My Brains, 141
My Teacher Is an Alien, 141

Nakano, Dokwhteli, 153
Native Americans, 158–60
Nature All Year Long, 97
Newspapers, 24
No Bake Cookies, recipe for, 132
Noble, Trinka Hakes, 77
Nonfiction materials, 20, 32
Norwegian Folk Tales, 103
Nutrition, 60, 75, 89, 98, 162

Occupations, 10
Older, Jules, 72
Organizations
    animal care, 79, 108
    disaster aid, 154
    environmental, 58, 105, 106, 113, 118, 135
    folklore society, 146

healthcare, 75, 155
    international, 87
    literacy promotion, 131
    marine, 108, 118
    tourism, 140
    tree related, 113, 114
Origami, 151, 153
Our Bodies, 151
Outside and Inside Trees, 114
Outside and Inside You, 151

Pallotta, Jerry, 63
Paper Magic: The Art of Paper Folding, 153
Parker, Nancy Winslow, 39
Parker, Steve, 67
Participatory comprehension, 16, 34
Paulos, Martha, illustrator, 46
Pen pals, 15, 38, 70, 87, 139
Penny, Malcom, 58
Petie, Harris, 112
Pets, 48, 56, 70, 77, 79, 93, 94
Petty, Kate, 58
Photographs
    of animal homes, 137
    of cloud patterns, 100
    over time, 51, 106, 114
    personal, 61, 133
Physical education (PE)
    bike rally, 87, 89
    body building, 120
    in bookweb, 36fig, 37
    games in, 71, 137, 160
    obstacle course, 101, 105
    orienteering, 116, 150, 164
    races, 49, 56, 62, 83, 146
    rope climbing, 53
    and sneakers, 68
    team sports, 86, 87, 92, 143, 145
    walking, 87, 112
Physical fitness, 14, 157
Pictograph, 13
Pittman, Helena Claret, 147
Plants
    growth of, 51, 95, 110, 128, 148, 159
    needs of, 51, 70
    rain forest, 111
    seed sprouting, 54, 55, 110, 114
    and transpiration, 51
Plaster of paris, 48, 143
Poems, 11, 46, 112
Polar Bear Alert (video), 58
Powers, William, 159
Prediction Cards, 20–21
Predictions, 17, 18, 20–21, 22, 23

Prelutsky, Jack, 81, 110
Pretzel Turtles, recipe for, 156
Pringle, Laurence, 40, 80
Puppets, 10, 37, 43, 89, 111
Puzzles, crossword, 11

Question generation, 16–18, 22, 23
Question writing
    on book content, 11, 12
    for games, 12, 14, 49
    for guest speaker, 12, 81
    as newswriters, 88
    for tests/quizzes, 4, 12
Quotations, 12

Rain forests, 106–8
Rainy Day, A, 97
Rambling Rose potpourri, 149
Ramona Quimby, Age 8, 138
Ramona the Pest, 138
Random House Book of Poetry for Children,
    110
Readers theatre, 72–74, 121–26
Reading
    in bookweb, 36fig, 38
    in curriculum, 7
    fostering enthusiasm for, 4–6
    in peer groups, 9
    and SMART questions, 17–18
    student perception of, 2
Reading centers, 11, 70
Recipes
    bean soup, 51-52
    black and white salad, 153
    flour dough (not edible), 55
    fudge, 156-57
    no-bake cookies, 132
    pretzel turtles, 156
    rambling rose, potpourri (not edible), 149
    yummy reptiles, 64
Recycling, 107, 115
Reed Jones, Carol, 114
Reflective Sharing Technique, 26–27
Reluctant readers
    and bookwebbing, 38
    expectations for, 6
    and motivation level, 2, 4, 38
    and participatory comprehension,
        16, 33
    positive environment for, 6
    strategies for, modeling, 18
Reptiles, 63–65, 77–79, 93–96,
    103, 142

Reptiles, 63
Resources, community, 38
    artists, 119
    coach/instructor, 120
    garden center/nursery, 113–14
    musicians, 116
    police station, 58
    senior citizens, 108
    storytellers, 102
Resources, expert, 12
    archaeologist, 81
    biologist/zoologist, 58, 81, 94
    county extension/farm bureau, 127
    healthcare providers, 75, 85, 89, 142, 152,
        154, 157
    herpetologist, 64, 94
    meteorologist, 98, 103, 159
    social scientist, 140
Reward systems, 1–2
Riddles, 12
Rock candy, recipe for, 148
Routines, bedtime, 88, 89
Royston, Angela, 151

Sadako and the Thousand Paper Cranes,
    151–54
Salamander Room, The, 25, 26, 93–96
Sanitation methods, 13, 162
Scary Stories to Tell in the Dark, 144
Schlein, Miriam, 81
Schwartz, Alvin, 144
Science. *See also* Living things
    Beaufort wind speed chart, 99, 103
    Bernoulli's principle, 91
    in bookweb, 36fig, 37
    electronics, 139
    mechanical devices, 66–67, 68
Science projects. *See also* Plants
    bird feeders, 47, 85
    brine shrimp, 118
    imaginary insect, 40
    rubber band car, 67
    terrariums, 43, 47, 61, 85, 107, 110–11
    weather station, 98–100
Scieszka, Jon, 121
Scrapbooks
    book content, 12
    family, 133
    human body, 154
    leaf collection, 148
    living things, 13, 48, 51, 145
    self history, 13
Seasons, and colors, 114
Secrets of the Wild Panda (video), 58

Seeds. *See* Plants
Self concept, 4
Semantic webbing, 22, 47, 103
Sequence determination, 6
Serengeti Diary (video), 85
Setting Continuum, 31–32
Shreve, Susan, 84
Simon, Seymour, 128
Singer, Marilyn, 156
Skeletons, 81–82, 142, 145
Skurzynski, Gloria, 147
Sky Tree, 113–16
Sleep habits, 88, 89
SMART (Student Motivated Active Reading
     Technique), 16–18
Snakes, Salamanders and Lizards, 63
Social groups, 41, 62, 69–71
Social studies, in bookweb, 36fig, 37
Soil, 70, 128
Song for the Ancient Forest, 114
Song of Stars, A: An Asian Legend, 116
Space Brat, 141
Spinelli, Jerry, 69
*Star Tales: North American Indian Stories
     About the Stars*, 116
States, 38, 83
Staub, Frank, 63
Steptoe, John, 109
Story creation
    on audiotapes, 46, 66
    epilogues, 141
    about living things, 40, 42, 113
    others' viewpoints in, 46, 50, 121
    rebus, 12
    rewriting, 66, 72, 144
    sequels, 12, 57, 77, 90, 93, 110, 161
    weather tall tales, 98
Storytelling, 15, 102
Student Generated Questions, 16–18
Student Motivated Active Reading Technique
    (SMART), 16–18
Substitute teacher, 90–92
Surprising Swimmers, 117–20

*Tadpole Tales and Other Totally Terrific
    Treats for Readers Theatre*, 72
Tadpoles and Frogs (video), 103
Tales of a Fourth Grade Nothing, 155–57
Taylor, Barbara, 67
Taylor, Theodore, 147
Teachers
    decision making by, 3
    as facilitators, 2–6
    modeling by, 4, 6, 18–19

Teaching quality, 5, 90
"Teaching to the mean," 6
Telephone book, 15
Television
    reporting for, 12, 15
    uses of, 52
Tests/quizzes, 4
*Thing at the Foot of the Bed and Other Scary
    Stories, The*, 144
Things That Go Bump in the Night, 144
Three Bears, The, 57–59
Time capsules, 14
Timelines, 12, 56, 67, 68, 103, 133
Titles, book, 12, 17, 155
Trading post, for books, 13
Traditional beliefs, 100–101, 116
Transparencies, 14
Transportation, 13, 139–40
Travel guides, 12, 86
Travel routes, 112, 154
Tree in the Ancient Forest, The, 114
Trees, 95, 106–8, 113–16
Trees, 114
True Story of the 3 Little Pigs, The,
    121–27
Tsuchiya, Yukion, 151
Turkle, Brinton, 147
Turtle Day, 156
Turtle in July, 156
Turtles, 156
Tutoring, 84
Tyrannosaurus Was a Beast, 81

Underachievers. *See* Reluctant readers
Usborne Book of Weather Facts, The, 159

Venn diagram, 142
Verbalization, 18–19
Very Hungry Caterpillar, The, 60–62
Videos, student, 10, 14, 58, 150, 152
Viking explorations, 105
Violent Earth, The (video), 130
Viorst, Judith, 66
Vocabulary, 20
Volcanoes, 128–30
Volcanoes, 128–30

Waber, Bernard, 88
Walton, Rick, 46
Way Things Work, The, 67
Weather, 159
Weather Forecasting, 24

Weather patterns
   regional, 13
   study of, 24–25, 97–101
   wind speed, 99, 103, 104, 159
Weather Words and What They Mean, 97
Weather Sky, The, 97
Web sites, 177–78
Wednesday Surprise, The, 131–34
Weiss, Harvey, 67
Wexo, John, 81
Whales, 118–19
*What Do You Say, Dear? A Book of Manners
   for All Occasions*, 157
What I Know, Want to Learn, Learned
   (K-W-L), 22–23
*What to Do When a Bug Climbs in Your
   Mouth*, 46
What Will the Weather Be?, 97
Where the Buffaloes Begin, 158–60
Whipping Boy, The, 161–64
Why Mosquitoes Buzz in People's Ears, 110
Why the Sun and the Moon Live in the Sky, 30
Wild Animals of Africa, 85

Wilder, Laura Ingalls, 9
Wilderness living, 147–50
Wilkins, Mary Jane, 159
Willard, Nancy, 103
Wiseman, Ann, 105
Word addition, 93-94
Word bank, 12
Wright, Joan Richards, 39
Writing. *See also* Story creation
   as abstract activity, 6
   adaptation, 11
   alternate version, 66
   guidebook for, 139
   for television, 12, 15

*X-Ray Picture Book of Everyday Things and
   How They Work, The*, 139

Yucky Reptile Alphabet Book, The, 63–65
Yummy Reptiles, recipe for, 64

About the Author

Anthony D. Fredericks

Tony's background includes extensive experience as a classroom teacher, curriculum coordinator, staff developer, author, professional storyteller, and university specialist in children's literature, language arts, and science education. In addition, Tony visits hundreds of schools and communities throughout North America working with educators, librarians, and children on effective literature-based learning strategies.

Tony has written more than 30 teacher resource books in a variety of areas, including the celebrated *Social Studies Through Children's Literature* (Teacher Ideas Press), the acclaimed *The Complete Guide to Thematic Units: Creating the Integrated Curriculum* (Christopher-Gordon), and the best-selling *The Complete Guide to Science Fairs* (Scott, Foresman) which he co-authored with Isaac Asimov.

Not only is Tony an advocate for the integration of children's literature throughout the lives of elementary children, he is also the author of such award-winning children's books as *Weird Walkers* (NorthWord), *Surprising Swimmers* (NorthWord), *Exploring the Rainforest* (Fulcrum), and *Clever Camouflagers* (NorthWord). He is currently a professor of education at York College in York, Pennsylvania, where he teaches methods courses in elementary education. Additionally, he conducts many national and international storytelling/writing workshops for teachers, librarians, and children each year.

SOCIAL STUDIES THROUGH CHILDREN'S LITERATURE: An Integrated Approach
Anthony D. Fredericks

This activity-centered approach to elementary social studies features children's picture books that illustrate important social studies concepts. Fredericks shows you how to make connections between social studies and literature and how to use book webbing. **Grades K–5**.
xviii, 192p. 8½x11 paper ISBN 0-87287-970-4

SCIENCE ADVENTURES WITH CHILDREN'S LITERATURE: A Thematic Approach
Anthony D. Fredericks

A must for all elementary science teachers! Focusing on the new National Science Teaching Standards, this activity-centered resource uses a variety of children's literature to integrate science across the elementary curriculum. **Grades K–3**.
xviii, 234p. 8½x11 paper ISBN 0-87287-667-5

TADPOLE TALES: Readers Theatre for Young Children
Anthony D. Fredericks

These wild and wacky adaptations of Mother Goose rhymes and traditional fairy tales will fill your classroom with laughter and learning! Featuring more than 25 reproducible scripts, an assortment of unfinished plays and titles, and practical guidelines for using readers theatre in the classroom, this book is a perfect resource for primary educators. **Grades 1–4**.
xii, 139p. 8½x11 paper ISBN 1-56308-547-X

STORYCASES: Book Surprises to Take Home
Richard Tabor and Suzanne Ryan

Increase your students' excitement about learning by extending the process with take-home project kits designed around book themes. An entertaining way to involve family members, and kids always love the novelty! **Grades K–2**.
xix, 161p. 8½x11 paper ISBN 1-56308-199-7

MAGIC MINUTES: Quick Read–Alouds for Every Day
Pat Nelson

Guaranteed to spread a special magic over listeners and bring many minutes of enchantment to all, this collection of short stories celebrates tried-and-true wisdom from around the world, as well as old-time humor and new-time heroes. **All levels**.
xv, 151p. paper ISBN 0-87287-996-8

For a FREE catalog or to place an order, please contact:

Teacher Ideas Press
Dept. B79 · P.O. Box 6633 · Englewood, CO 80155-6633
1-800-237-6124, ext. 1 · Fax: 303-220-8843 · E-mail: lu-books@lu.com

Check out our TIP Web site!
www.lu.com/tip